NORTHERN MEMORIES

More high-spirited tales of
"Growing Up North"

by Jerry Harju

NORTHERN MEMORIES

More high-spirited tales of
"Growing Up North"

by Jerry Harju

Cover Design by Stacey Willey and Mark Nowicki
Editing by Pat Green and Karen Murr

Copyright 2002
Jerry Harju

Published by North Harbor Publishing
Marquette, Michigan

Publishing Coordination by
Globe Printing, Inc.
Ishpeming, Michigan

Printed by Sheridan Books, Ann Arbor, Michigan

ISBN 0-9670205-7-3
Library of Congress Control Number 2001098752

April 2002

Introduction

In the early 1990's I started my writing career with a series of short stories about my misadventures growing up in Michigan's Upper Peninsula. These were published in three books: *Northern Reflections, Northern D'Lights,* and *Northern Passages.* I've written other books since, but the demand for these first three remains robust. People have often asked when I would write another book in the "Northern" series. Well, here it is.

In *Northern Memories* I've tried to capture entertaining and nostalgic snapshots of life in the late 1930's and '40's, the time I was growing up. Our family, like most people we knew, were poor, but we didn't know it. (Okay, maybe my parents knew it, but I didn't.) Many aspects of our daily life back then were primitive by today's standards. I hope you'll find this journey back in time an enjoyable trip.

Yeah, that's me on the cover. Cute kid, wasn't I?

Jerry Harju
North Harbor Publishing
528 E. Arch St.
Marquette, MI 49855
Toll Free: (877) 906-3984
E-mail: jharju@chartermi.net
Website: jerryharju.com

Dedication

To my Uncle Arvid Olander, who taught me many things.

Acknowledgements

Putting a book together requires the time and effort of several very talented people. I especially thank my long-time editors, sweetheart Pat Green and cousin Karen Murr, who once again put the final professional polish to my writing. Stacey Willey and Mark Nowicki did an excellent job on the cover design. Alex Stiritz cleverly beat out several other people in the contest to come up with an appropriate title, and Steve Schmeck was kind enough to produce the bar codes for the cover. Other folks–Jeff (a.k.a. Kippy) Jacobs, Lidia Menchaca, Dr. Bruce Pavlov (my dentist), and "Ike" Isaacson (my Model A Ford expert)–willingly reviewed the story manuscripts for technical accuracy. My aunt, Martha Byttyla, also provided valuable background information. Sadly, she passed away before the book got into print.

Table of Contents

Books by Jerry Harju

The Driving Lesson

*D*riving a car is easy nowadays. You simply touch the steering wheel with one finger, and the power steering takes over. You don't even have to shift gears anymore—the automatic transmission does that. You do have to wake up your right foot occasionally to tap the brake pedal, disengaging the cruise control so the computerized anti-lock braking system can slow the car. Your left foot is just along for the ride.

It certainly wasn't like that when I learned to drive. With the early, primitive automobiles you literally had to overpower the jalopy to show it who was boss. My first car was a 1930 Model A Ford. Driving that car required the strength of Charles Atlas and the equivalent of a masters degree in mechanical engineering.

One particular episode yells out to be told. During the winter of 1950 we were living in Republic, Michigan, in the U.P. One Saturday morning I was driving my parents to my grandmother's house. . .

Two hundred yards from Chub Mattila's Standard gas station I began to slow the Model A down. Considering the shape the brakes were in, stopping the car required a lot of advanced planning.

"Whaddaya goin' in here for?" my old man asked.

I pulled into the station next to the pumps. "I'm almost outta gas, Pop. You got any money?"

"Again? Fer crissake, you were almost outta gas the last time I climbed into this thing. What happened to the gas I bought last week?"

"Fifteen cents worth doesn't go far, Pop. That's not even a gallon." Of course, my car never *had* more than a gallon in the tank at any one time. If I'd ever had enough money to fill up the tank, the old clunker would've swooned with ecstasy.

During my three-months of Model A ownership, just to keep the heap running, I'd had to replace gaskets, generator brushes, radiator hoses, the fan belt, and disassemble and clean the carburetor, not to mention pounding out a dented brake drum after a wheel had fallen off at thirty miles an hour. I'd fixed the driver's-side window so it could roll down because I had high hopes that someday I'd be able to take the car to the big city of Marquette, where I'd need to stick my arm out the window to make turn signals in the heavy traffic.

The old man grumbled, but after poking around in his leather coin purse for a few seconds, he dug out a quarter and handed it to me.

Chub Mattila strolled out to the gas pump, wiping his hands on a greasy rag. Without a word he lifted the hood, pulled out the dipstick, and showed me the oil level.

"A quart low, like last week. Yer in luck, though. I just got some good used stuff this morning. Took it out of old man Anderson's new Buick. Oil's got only 2000 miles on it. Give it to ya for a dime a quart."

I handed him the quarter. "Yeah, gimme a quart and fifteen cents worth of regular." This was my weekly gas-station transaction, three quarts of gasoline and one quart of used oil.

"Wait a minute," the old man said. "You ain't even gettin' a quarter's worth of gas?"

"The car needs oil," I explained. Never having driven, my father had no idea of what it cost to maintain a car.

Chub put in the quart of oil and then, with practiced eye-hand coordination, delicately pumped in fifteen cents worth of gasoline.

I pulled back onto the snow-covered street and headed toward my grandmother's house.

My mother leaned forward from her customary position in the back seat and watched what I was doing. "How hard can this be?"

"How hard can *what* be?" my father asked.

"Learning how to drive a car."

"It's easy," I said offhandedly as I expertly weaved the car back and forth to stay on the dribble of sand that the Republic Township truck had deposited on the icy street earlier that morning.

"Can you teach me?" she asked me.

The old man turned around and stared at her in disbelief. "Teach you what? How to *drive*?"

"Why not?"

"Yer too old to learn how to drive," the old man declared.

My mother bristled at that. "I'm not even fifty."

"It's easy, Ma," I said. "I can show you how to drive in no time, even if you *are* getting up in years."

"You stay out of this."

Now the old man took a different tack with my mother. "None of yer sisters drive. They get around pretty good."

"They get around when their *husbands* decide to drive them around. Jerry will be going off to college soon. You can't teach me to drive because the only thing *you've* ever driven was a team of horses. I don't intend to be a pedestrian for the rest of my life."

"I dunno," the old man continued. "I been watchin' the kid drive this car, an' it looks pretty tricky to me."

Growing more agitated, she leaned forward from the back seat, jerking her thumb toward me while she jawed angrily at my father. "If *he* can learn how to drive this car, *I* can learn how to drive it."

The following Saturday my mother was ready for her driving lesson. I'd never in my life taught anyone anything. Nobody wanted to learn any of my valuable skills, like how to trap and skin a weasel, for instance. For years my mother had been trying to pound all sorts of knowledge into *my* head whether I liked it or not, and now I was looking forward to teaching *her* something for a change.

That morning I took the car battery from its overnight storage in my bedroom and lugged it out to the Model A parked in the backyard.

My mother, bundled up against the cold, stood by and watched me install the battery beneath the Ford's floorboards. "Why do you keep taking the battery in the house every night?"

"The cold weather. If I leave it in the car, it's dead in the morning. Won't have to do that in the summer, though."

"Do other people do that?"

"No, but this battery is shot. If we had a new one, we could leave it in the car overnight." I'd purposely used the word "we," hoping that if she was going to seriously take up driving, then a new battery would rightfully become a family investment.

I attached the cables to the battery and tried to start the car. The old battery turned the engine over a few times but quickly went dead. No surprise. In fact, it would have been a surprise if the car had started.

Since my mother was expressing such a keen interest in driving, I decided that she'd better know how to get the car started when the battery was dead. This was an ideal opportunity to show her how.

"Sometimes you haf'ta crank the engine to get 'er started, Ma. Before you do that, though, you gotta make sure the ignition is turned on. Then you pull out the choke, set the spark advance and the throttle. Oh, and one more thing, don't forget to put the gearshift in neutral. You don't want to get run over by your own car when you're out there in front, cranking it, heh, heh, heh."

My mother failed to see the humor in that. She stared at me like I was speaking Chinese.

I took care of all of the precranking settings, then grabbed the crank and inserted it into the crank hole below the radiator. One obstacle to manually cranking a Model A was the heavy iron bumper jutting out a foot in front of the crank opening.

I motioned for my mother to step up and watch closely. "You haf'ta straddle the bumper with your legs, like this, Ma, so you can get a good grip on the crank handle. And you'll probably have to hike up your dress, cause the bumper's kind of high for you."

She looked at the bumper and crank, looked at me, and then laughed hysterically. That's good, I thought. She was suddenly realizing that driving could be lots of fun.

The motor oil was stiff from the cold, and I grunted with exertion as I began turning the engine over with the crank. On the third attempt, one of the four cylinders suddenly fired. . .but only once. The crank viciously snapped back counterclockwise—a common problem with cranking a Model A engine—and the spiteful machine made a serious attempt to pull my thumb out of its socket. I dropped my leather chopper in the snow, and in my usual fashion hopped around, sucking on the stricken thumb.

"It's okay, Ma," I said, chuckling good-naturedly to show that it really didn't hurt. "This happens all the time."

My mother said, "Learning how to drive is one thing, but if you think for one minute that I'm going to get out in the snow and break my fingers cranking this car, you've got another think coming. I'll leave that job to you."

The engine fired up after a couple more cranks, and we climbed in the car with me behind the wheel. I was going to take us out to an appropriate place to begin the driving lesson. On the outskirts of Republic, along the Michigamme River, a narrow two-lane road followed the winding river for miles. Few people lived there. With virtually no traffic it was an ideal place for a driving lesson. Also, my mother had made it clear that she wasn't quite ready to have any of the local women see her behind the wheel of this rattletrap.

I drove up the river road a few miles to charge up the battery, then stopped and turned off the ignition. "Okay, Ma, you ready?"

My mother, normally a take-charge person, wasn't too sure now, but she nodded and we switched places.

The Model A's front seats were securely bolted to the wooden floorboards with no adjustment features. My mother, only five-foot-three, couldn't reach the brake and clutch pedals with her feet.

She glared down at the pedals. "What kind of stupid car is this?"

"Try sitting on the edge of the seat so you can reach."

She did that, then nervously tapped the pedals with both feet.

"Okay, now you're gonna start the car. First push in the clutch."

"Clutch? What's a clutch?"

"That pedal on the left."

"What does it do?"

"It's there so the engine can grab the wheels and make the car go." That statement basically covered my total knowledge of automobile clutches.

She pushed in the clutch with her foot.

"No, Ma, use your left foot."

"What difference does it make?"

"You're gonna need your right foot for the brake and the gas."

"You mean to tell me I'm going to have to do all that at the same time?"

"Well, yeah, but you'll get the hang of it in no time."

She pushed in the clutch with her left foot. "Now what?"

"Okay, now you increase the spark advance, adjust the throttle, and pull out the choke." I showed her where all the levers and knobs were located.

"All that and I haven't even started the car yet?"

"It's easy, Ma. You're going to start it right now. Turn the key on and press the starter button with your right toe." I pointed at the starter button located near the gas pedal.

She turned the ignition key and hit the starter with her foot. The car leapt forward like a bucking bronco and then, just as suddenly, stopped.

"Ma, I told you to push in the clutch, remember? The car was in first gear."

My mother fumbled around for her glasses which had fallen to the floorboards when the car bucked. She put them back on. "You didn't tell me to *keep* it in."

Still intent on giving a good driving lesson, I began the whole start-up procedure again. "Okay, set the spark advance halfway, open the throttle up a quarter, pull out the choke, push in the clutch with your left foot, turn on the ignition, and press the starter with your right toe."

She looked confused, and I couldn't imagine why. My instructions were crystal clear.

I talked her through it again, and this time she got it right, but the aged battery had gotten tired of waiting. The starter let out one feeble moan and lapsed into silence.

I got out of the car. "Well, the battery's dead again. I'll have to crank it."

"I don't want you even *thinking* about driving this bucket of bolts to another town," my mother warned.

I manually cranked the engine a few times, and this time it started right up. I climbed in the passenger seat. "Okay, Ma, push in the clutch and put it in first gear." I showed her the position for the gearshift lever. "Now, let the clutch out slowly and give it some gas."

"Give it some gas?"

"Press on the gas pedal."

It didn't work the first time, or the second time, because she kept killing the engine, and I had to get out and recrank it after each attempt. The third time she let the clutch out successfully. With a rattling "bucketa, bucketa, bucketa," the Model A surged forward.

"Omigawd," my mother cried. "What do I do now?"

"Steer away from that tree you're going to hit," I advised quickly.

She jerked the steering wheel to the left, but nothing happened.

"Brake! Brake!" I yelled.

At the very last split second she managed to locate the brake pedal. With the rear wheels locked, the car began to skid, at the same time hopping forward like a crazed rabbit because the clutch wasn't in. We finally bucked and slid to a stop inches away from a very large pine tree on the side of the road.

We sat there for a moment in silence. Then my mother uttered some very unladylike phrases about the steering wheel not working.

"Sure, it works, Ma. I guess I forgot to tell you. The steering wheel's got a little slop in it."

"Slop?"

"There's a worm gear connecting the steering column to the front-wheel linkage. The gear's pretty worn, and that's why there's slop in the steering wheel. But it still works. You just have to move it back and forth a lot, like this." I twisted the wheel a full ninety degrees and then back to show her what I meant. "Once you get the hang of it, it's real easy."

"How much did you pay for this pile of junk?"

"Ninety dollars. A great buy, eh?"

"Oh, yes. A great buy."

I cranked up the engine again and got back in. My mother, perched precariously on the edge of the seat, carefully let the clutch out, and the car began to move.

"Left! Left!" I screamed as the car veered toward the right-hand snowbank.

She whipped the steering wheel a hard 180 degrees to the left, and the car shot across the road, directly toward another snowbank.

"Right! Right!"

She twisted the wheel to the right, and the Model A cut across the road toward the snowbank on the other side.

"Left! Left!"

"For crying out loud, make up your mind!"

She finally gained some semblance of control, but the car still zigzagged crazily down the road with the engine roaring in first gear.

"It's time to shift gears, Ma."

"Shift gears?"

"You have to shift into higher gears to make the car go faster."

The car was now narrowly missing the high snowbanks on both sides of the road as she continued pulling the steering wheel back and forth. "Are you crazy? It's going too fast now!"

"You gotta learn how to shift gears, Ma. Put in the clutch and then push the gearshift lever up and over to the right, into second gear." I reached over and touched the vibrating, floor-mounted shift lever and made a motion with my hand. "You shove it up here to get the car into second gear."

She put the clutch in and made a concerted but fortunately unsuccessful effort to shift from low into reverse gear. In the process the transmission got several gear teeth ground into hamburger.

"No, no, that's reverse. Second gear is over here." I rammed the shift into second. "Now, let out the clutch again." She did, and the Model A bucked forward in second gear, moving faster.

"Okay, that's good. Now, push the clutch in again and pull the gearshift straight down. That'll be high gear."

"I don't *want* to go in high gear," she wailed above the motor noise, but finally did as I instructed.

"Now, let the clutch out, and you'll be in high gear."

She let the clutch out, and that's when things really began happening. The car sped up and threw her backward into the seat, her feet flying clear of the pedals. At the same time, her right hand slipped off the steering wheel and rammed the throttle lever on the steering column into a wide-open position. The engine howled and the Model A shot forward at top speed.

"Brakes! Brakes!" I yelled.

"I can't *reach* the brakes!"

I thrust my foot over, trying to reach the brake pedal, but just then the car sideswiped a roadside snowbank, knocking me into the passenger's-side door. I yelled at her to turn off the ignition, but she couldn't hear me above the noise of her own screams.

I again tried to reach the controls, but the speeding car suddenly bounced off the snowbank on the other side of the road. I crashed into my mother as her screams shifted into a higher octave.

With the engine roaring at full throttle, the Model A shot back and forth across the road, ricochetting from snowbank to snowbank like a billiard ball. I managed to slap the throttle lever closed just before the car slammed into a final snowbank head on. A mountain of snow cascaded onto the hood and windshield. The engine was still running—the back tires spinning and throwing up geysers of snow behind us.

I reached over and turned the engine off, then jumped out and inspected the fenders and radiator. Hugely relieved, I reported, "Good news, Ma. The car's okay. I'll just clear the snow off the windshield, and we'll try 'er again."

My mother adjusted her upper dentures which had shaken loose during the final impact. Finally, when she was able to talk, she said quietly, "Take me home."

The following Saturday as I was driving my mother and the old man to the post office I again pulled into the Standard station, whipping the steering wheel vigorously back and forth to avoid hitting the gas pumps.

"Whut, y'need gas again?" the old man growled. "I could hire a taxi cheaper if we had a taxi in this town."

"We burned up a lot of gas when I was trying to teach Ma how to drive," I explained. No one had bothered to tell him about the outcome of the driving lesson.

"She did that much driving?"

"Well, sort of. You see, what happened was . . ."

My mother interrupted by reaching forward from the back seat and pressing two dollar bills in my hand. "Just fill up the gas tank and keep your mouth shut."

Frankenstein and the Chicken

One summer morning in 1940 my pal, Kippy Jacobs, who lived across the railroad tracks, barged into our kitchen and slumped into a chair at the linoleum-covered table where I was eating breakfast.

I laid my spoon down and burped. After a fourth bowl of Wheaties, I was grateful for the interruption to let the milk and cereal settle into the lower recesses of my overburdened digestive system.

Kippy looked at my bowl of Wheaties disapprovingly. "Don' ya put anything on it? I put peaches on mine."

I shook my head. I couldn't afford to load up the cereal with fruit while trying to finish off a whole box in one sitting. Kippy just didn't appreciate the logistics of acquiring box tops.

The Wheaties-box-top crisis came up unexpectedly when Jack Armstrong had broadcast an urgent message, warning all of his young radio listeners that his offer for the mysterious Egyptian Whistle Ring would expire in three days.

I had to have that ring. The hulking eight- and nine-year-old Catholic kids in Ishpeming thought nothing of pounding up on an unwary seven-year-old Lutheran, and I needed some real protection. I could blow coded blasts on the whistle ring and my pals would rush to the rescue. The Wheaties box top had to be sent in immediately, but my mother had issued an ironclad edict. No box top would be put into the mail until the cereal box was empty. In order to meet Jack Armstrong's deadline I had to polish off the entire box of Wheaties that morning.

Kippy thrust a theater flyer in my face. "Quit eatin' already and look at the Saturday shows."

The glossy brochure, stuffed into mailboxes every Monday morning, advertised the weekly movie fare. Most important was the Saturday-matinee listing. Every Saturday afternoon, come rain, shine, sleet, or snow, Kippy and I trucked down to the Ishpeming Theater on Cleveland Avenue and immersed ourselves into an electrifying five-hour extravaganza of nonstop, shoot-em-up action. Forty-five-caliber bullets flew as thick as swarms of Upper Michigan mosquitoes. Scores of black-hatted mustachioed bad guys were socked, rocked, and wounded (but never killed), generally receiving their comeuppance from the likes of Gene Autry, Roy Rogers, Charles Starrett, Ken Maynard, Hopalong Cassidy, and Tex Ritter. These clean-living, fast-shooting, guitar-picking cowboy heroes were always assisted by comical sidekicks who, through their own bumbling, usually wound up in the clutches of the villains. Naturally, the rescue was pulled off by the cowboy star, or sometimes even by the star's horse. Roy Rogers' horse, Trigger, with an IQ well over 200, often rounded up the crooks all by himself, not trusting Roy to do the job.

I turned to the Saturday movies on the back of the brochure. "Hey, ya see this? *Spoilers of the Range* with Charles Starrett!"

Kippy smirked. "Yeah, but look at the second show."

The second feature was *Frankenstein*.

The Ishpeming Theater provided a steady diet of westerns on Saturday afternoons, but every so often they'd throw in a horror movie.

The breakfast milk curdled in my stomach. I hated horror movies.

Kippy, of course, knew this and grinned wickedly when he asked, "Ya gonna go or are ya gonna chicken out?"

"Sure I'm gonna go," I replied without conviction.

Kippy chortled, getting a big kick out of this. "Ya almost fainted at *The Phantom Creeps* show. Ya looked worse than the phantom."

"I ate too many licorice sticks that Saturday."

"How about the time we saw *Revenge of the Zombies*? Ya jumped outta a yer seat an' took off for the lobby like yer pants wuz on fire."

He was right. During a horror movie, I'd often panic and bolt for the lobby to try to get a grip on my nerves.

"Well, okay, mebbe I used t'get a li'l scared," I admitted offhandedly. "I wuz a little kid then."

Kippy smiled knowingly and ran off to lay some nails on the railroad tracks before the midmorning ore train came by. I resumed eating Wheaties, but my heart wasn't in it. The upcoming Frankenstein movie had curtailed my appetite.

Every Friday evening the arduous ritual of extracting matinee money from my father took place. Precise timing was the key. Right after supper the old man was always in a mellow mood with a full stomach. That night he was sitting in his living-room rocker in front of our fifty-six-tube Zenith radio, rolling his after-dinner cigarette, and preparing to listen to "The Fred Allen Show."

"Pop, I need some money for the show tomorrow."

The old man paused rolling the Bull Durham cigarette. He had a number of standard responses to my request, and I knew them all. Tonight he employed the sister routine. "Money? Yer sister never asked fer show money."

That was true. Esther, nine years my senior and a clever

entrepreneur, had scoured the Ishpeming alleys for empty bottles to sell to the moonshiners, thereby financing her Saturday matinee ticket. But this was 1940. The moonshine market had dried up.

"Nobody buys old bottles anymore," I told him.

The old man immediately shifted his strategy to test my endurance. "Why don'cha try sellin' rhubarb?"

"I did that. Nobody wanted it, remember?"

During the summer, rhubarb grew in profusion in our backyard, and last year I'd hit on the brilliant idea of making a killing in the rhubarb market. My mother helped me make a sign, "PIE PLANT 1 PENNY." I nailed it to an old orange crate filled with cut rhubarb stalks and set up business in front of our house. Too soon I learned a brutal lesson in the law of supply and demand. No one on our street ever bought rhubarb for the simple reason that everyone had a backyard full of the stuff.

The old man began fiddling with the radio dial to find Fred Allen. "How much ya need?" He knew the exact amount to the penny since we'd go through this routine every week, but he enjoyed playing the game.

"A dime."

He always arched his eyebrows way up when I said that. "A dime? You know how long it takes me to earn a dime?"

Since I had yet to be schooled in higher mathematics, I naturally didn't know, so I always shook my head.

"I thought the show was a nickel. Why do ya need a dime?" He knew the answer to that, too.

"Five cents for candy."

"Candy? Candy'll rot yer teeth. Most of 'em are yer second teeth. Ya don't get any more. Take an apple from the house."

The moment was now at hand to don my most sorrowful, on-the-verge-of-tears expression, twist around with my hands behind my back, and beg. *"Pulleese?"*

The ritual was complete. The old man reached into his pocket and took out a dime. "Sum day you'll haf'ta get yer own dimes."

Early Saturday afternoon Kippy and I were throwing elbows in Linna's Drugstore with a dozen or so other young theatergoers, jockeying for position in front of the candy-display case. This matinee-preliminary consumed at least a half-hour since five cents bought a substantial amount of candy, and careful selection was necessary to make certain that your purchase lasted the entire matinee.

Clyde Maki, an acne-scarred teenager who worked for old man Linna, stood behind the candy case, glowering at the mob of kids as he filled shouted orders.

"How many malted-milk balls kin I get fer a penny?"

"Four, same as last Saturday."

"Will ya gimme ten fer two cents?"

Clyde sneered. "Don't they teach arithmetic anymore? Four times two is eight, not ten."

I stood there, undecided. Licorice sticks were my favorite, but the licorice had to be fresh. Eating old licorice was like chewing on rope.

"Kin I touch the licorice?" I asked.

Clyde Maki leaned over the top of the candy case, getting into my face. "You can touch the licorice when you buy it."

"But how do I know it ain't old an' tough?" I objected.

Clyde snatched a licorice stick out of the case and neatly bit off half of it, lodging it in his cheek. "Fresh enough for ya?"

Seeing this, Kippy chimed in. "Kin I have the other half of that piece?"

Clyde snorted at the audacity of Kippy's question and shoved the remaining licorice into his already bulging cheek.

But the demonstration sold me. "Gimme two licorice sticks."

Another favorite of mine was "sweet pops." The miniature soda-pop bottles were made from translucent wax filled with an ultra-sweet syrup that dissolved tooth enamel on contact. Sweet pops were an excellent investment because after all the syrup was sucked out, the wax bottle could be chewed throughout the remainder of the matinee.

The regular sweet-pop flavors were orange and strawberry, but today I spotted a new one.

"What's that?" I asked Clyde, pointing to a green sweet pop.

"Lime."

"What's lime?"

Clyde didn't have time for useless small talk and moved off to fill orders from kids who didn't require extensive background information on the candy.

He finally came back. "Look, you want them sweet pops or not?"

"What's lime?" I asked again.

"Hey, it's like lemon, only green, okay?"

I spent two cents on four lime pops and blew my last penny on four malted-milk balls. Clutching our investments, Kippy and I rushed off to get in line for the matinee.

Bunzy McNamara, the Ishpeming Theater manager, ran a tight ship on Saturday afternoons. Before the show began, he took his first tactical position just inside the lobby door, deftly snatching tickets from the outstretched hands of the thundering herd as they galloped in from the box office. At the same time he ran a practiced eye over each ticket holder, looking for suspicious bulges that might turn out to be iron-ore chunks, pop bottles, or other lethal objects that could be hurled from the balcony. Moments later Bunzy would be stationed up in the balcony, guarding the fire-exit door to make certain that no one in the theater was sneaking in friends standing outside on the fire escape. During the matinee he patrolled the theater aisles, keeping order among the unruly young cowboys, whacking the more violent ones into submission, and in extreme cases yanking a wrongdoer out of his seat and escorting him to the exit.

Kippy and I handed Bunzy our tickets and made our way to the balcony. Many kids preferred the main floor, especially the front row right up next to the screen, within grabbing distance of the bad guys. Kippy and I liked the balcony—safer since it was the launching point and not the impact area for various missiles thrown during the heat of battle.

We picked our way across the gum-encrusted balcony floor to our favorite seats. The theater filled up, and the atmosphere began to radiate a gamy ambience of unwashed bodies; weekly baths weren't on the agenda until that night.

The long, burgundy-velvet stage curtain parted, and the house lights dimmed—the kickoff for the Saturday matinee. Raucous cheers erupted from the crowd.

The familiar Paramount crowing rooster led off the newsreel. Empty candy boxes were hurled toward the stage. The newsreel held little interest for us. After all, who could work up a sweat over a little German guy with a funny mustache?

A *Pete Smith Specialty* was next, a short reeler featuring funnyman Pete Smith, who as usual introduced an assortment of exotic animals, this time an elephant, a llama, and a hyena who all proved to be considerably smarter than Pete.

A string of cartoons featuring Bugs Bunny, Elmer Fudd, and others, bashing each other fast and furiously, set the tempo for the first movie.

Spoilers of the Range adhered to the usual time-honored,

horse-opera script. Bad guys were rustling cattle from an honest, hard-working rancher who just so happened to have a beautiful daughter. The other variation of the old shoot-em-ups was when the villains already *had* the cattle and were waging war on an honest, hard-working *sheep* rancher who just so happened to have a beautiful daughter.

For a solid spine-tingling sixty minutes Charles Starrett—steely eyed and lantern-jawed—traded hot lead with the lowdown rustlers. Ranchers and rustlers alike used magic six-shooters that enabled you to blast off at least twenty rounds without reloading. When the bad guys finally ran out of ammunition, they threw their empty guns at Starrett. I always wondered why they did that.

Charles Starrett was my favorite cowboy because he didn't sing. Gene Autry, Roy Rogers, and Tex Ritter would have fared a lot better at rounding up crooks if they hadn't been compelled to break into song at the slightest provocation. If they'd just sung to cattle to calm them at night, it would've been okay, but they serenaded *women* of all things.

Starrett casually polished off a root beer in a saloon and then proceeded to get into a knock-down, drag-out fight with several burly town ruffians. Without fail, all of the saloon furniture got broken up in the process. It was never clear to me who paid for all of the damage.

As the story moved on, Starrett surprised the rustlers in an abandoned sawmill just as they were about to slice up his bumbling sidekick with a large power saw.

Spoilers of the Range drew to a close with Charles Starrett, mounted atop his prancing white stallion, riding off into the sunset with the cattle-rancher's beautiful daughter. And that was another thing I couldn't figure out; where did the cowboy heroes take these women at the end of the movie? And why?

Daffy Duck was squeezed in between the two main features. I

tried to concentrate on the cartoon but couldn't. My mind now dwelt feverishly on the upcoming second feature. *Would I have enough guts to watch Frankenstein through to the end, or would I panic and run?*

The *Frankenstein* movie began. Made in 1931, it had a few miles on it, but none of the movies we saw at the Ishpeming Theater were new. The management saw no need to show first-run films to a pack of grubby children.

The opening scene was a graveyard at night. The worn sound track hissed ominously as Dr. Frankenstein and Fritz, his malformed, demented assistant, lurked behind a large boulder, waiting for the gravedigger to finish placing the last few shovelfuls of dirt on a fresh grave. The malted-milk ball in my mouth turned to chalk. No one had to tell me what was coming next.

After digging up the corpse and hauling it up to their laboratory in an old abandoned stone windmill, Dr. Frankenstein dispatched Fritz to a medical school to steal a brain.

The whole theater fell silent. Kippy, his eyes riveted to the screen, had an unchewed licorice stick hanging out of the corner of his mouth. I eyeballed the distance between my seat and the balcony stairs.

In no time the doctor and his fiendish assistant had hauled a large array of dangerous-looking electrical equipment into the laboratory and had it all hooked up and plugged in. Fat arcs of electricity snapped, crackled, and popped as they snaked across stout metal electrodes housed in huge glass spheres. Lights on control panels blinked impatiently. Mysterious concoctions bubbled in chemical beakers, sending toxic vapors up into the flickering shadows in the windmill tower.

On a long metal gurney in the center of the laboratory lay something draped in heavy gray cloth. It had the distinct outline of a very large body. The tented cloth at one end indicated it must be wearing size 24 EEEEE shoes.

I gripped the armrests of my seat, eyeing the stairs again.

A violent thunderstorm was rattling the delicate laboratory apparatus, but the weather suited Dr. Frankenstein just fine. He explained to Fritz that they were going to give life to whatever it was on the table by hitting it with a bolt of lightning. Fritz grinned fiendishly and nodded.

Lightning flashed across the shabby walls of the Ishpeming theater as the two madmen proceeded with their experiment. At the most critical moment, just as a lightning bolt zapped the newly implanted brain on the gurney, there was a sudden pounding on the old windmill door.

Dr. Frankenstein's fiancée, a baby-faced, beautiful young blonde, had arrived to talk to him about going back to America for their forthcoming wedding.

The audience tensed. The blonde was in extreme danger, and several kids yelled at her to get the heck out of there.

Yet she stayed, which figured, of course. Any woman wanting to marry a crackpot like Dr. Frankenstein must have had a few screws loose herself.

The next scene was the moment I'd been dreading. The monster, now upright and alive—well, sort of alive—stumbled out of a dungeon adjacent to the laboratory. It gazed around with dead-man eyes set beneath a prominent, overhanging, wide forehead that had a coarsely stitched, long jagged incision where the stolen criminal's brain had been implanted. It's lipless mouth formed a trace of an evil smile as it lurched forward.

It was coming for me.

I don't actually recall getting out of my seat, but I *do* remember tromping on the shoes of a dozen kids as I clawed my way down the row toward the stairway.

Of course, everyone in the balcony saw this. Tommy LaBrut, the legendary South-Ishpeming bully, popped out of his seat and stood in front of me at the head of the stairs, flapping his arms like a chicken.

"Where ya goin', chicken? Did Frankenstein scare the li'l chicken? Lookit the chicken run, you guys!"

His cronies took up the cry, flapping their arms and cackling mercilessly as I stumbled down the stairs.

I stood trembling in the empty lobby, trying to suppress the squeaky whimpers leaking from my mouth. I was grateful that no one was around to witness my sad breakdown. I would have gone home, but I was determined to stay for *The Green Archer* serial coming on after *Frankenstein*.

The Saturday matinee always concluded with the latest weekly episode of a serial where the hero starts out by miraculously extricating himself from a certain-death predicament to resume his pursuit of evildoers. Yet, at the end of the reel he would somehow find himself in an equally lethal fix—a shallow ploy to lure us back into the theater the following Saturday. And it always worked. The previous week the Green Archer was about to be crushed between two beds of sharp spikes, and I had to find out if he was going to get out alive.

I was standing in the middle of the deserted lobby, biding my time, wishing I hadn't left my candy in the balcony, when I heard a squeaky female voice behind me.

"You scared, too?"

Bridgett O'Toole was the last person I wanted to see right then. Bridgett, the Jezebel of the second-grade at Central School, had yet to find a boy that she didn't like. Whenever the mood struck her she would bushwhack some unsuspecting young male in the cloakroom and plant a big wet kiss on his cheek before he knew what was happening.

"I saw ya goin' down the stairs, so I followed you," Bridgett chirped merrily, giving me a predatory leer as she positioned herself between me and the men's room, cutting off my best avenue of escape.

"Wanna a Tootsie Roll?" she said, holding out her sack of candy. "I got lots."

I reluctantly took a Tootsie Roll. I didn't want to encourage her, but I desperately needed something to calm my nerves.

"I'm not going back in there," Bridgett said. "That Frankenstein scares me."

"Uh-huh," I mumbled. It was hard to believe that *anything* scared Bridgett.

She coyly fingered one of her long red curls. "You wanna come over to my house? I got some new Shirley Temple paper dolls."

Playing with paper dolls—what a disgusting idea. "No," I said.

"I think I got some cowboy paper dolls, too."

A bald-faced lie. There was no such thing as cowboy paper dolls.

"You ever kiss a girl?" Bridgett asked.

"Heck, no."

She moved in closer, smiling seductively at me, revealing a large chunk of Tootsie Roll wedged in the gap between her two front teeth.

"You wanna kiss *me*?"

I leaped back in fright. "You kiddin'?"

Bridgett reached out and grabbed my arm. "Well, I wanna kiss *you*!"

I tried to pry her off my arm, but Bridgett had a grip of steel. Slowly, she reeled me in, puckering her lips in anticipation of a big smooch. I looked wildly around the lobby, but there wasn't a soul in sight. Where was Bunzy when I needed him?

Panic-stricken, I began swatting her with my free hand, but it had no effect.

Bridgett giggled. "You're not supposed to hit girls." Her face, close now, was blurring in my vision. The smell of stale Tootsie Rolls coiled out on her hot, steamy breath.

I stomped my foot down sharply on her toes and did it a second time for good measure. Yelping in pain, Bridgett began hopping on one foot and finally let go of my arm.

I took off up the balcony stairs.

"I'll get you!" she hollered.

Breathless, I sat back down in my seat. Kippy had my bag of candy in his lap, happily munching on one of my licorice sticks.

"I thought you went home," he said guiltily, handing the bag back.

"I just went to the toilet," I lied. Sorely needing a drink, I bit the top off of one of my lime pops and drained the contents in one gulp. I glanced over at the stairs, but Bridgett hadn't followed me.

The movie had progressed to where the mad doctor's fiancêe had somehow convinced him to have the wedding in the village near the laboratory. But just before the ceremony, the monster, now on the loose, had come in through her bedroom window just as she was zipping up her bridal gown and was now chasing her around the room while she screamed her head off.

Hey, I thought, this wasn't such a bad movie after all. The monster had the right idea. If he caught the woman, it served her right for butting into the mad doctor's business. Girls always did dumb things like that.

"*Get 'er!*" I yelled to Frankenstein.

The Camp

Glenn eyeballed the distance. "She ain't gonna reach, needs a coupl'a more links."

"Keep it down," I whispered. The cemetary was on the edge of town. While the closest house was over two hundred yards away, voices could carry in the still morning air, and our operation was extremely covert.

Glenn Brown and I were gently holding one end of a dandelion chain up off the gravel roadway, trying to make it reach the iron eyelet sunk in one of the concrete gate pillars at the entrance to the Republic cemetery. The other end of the chain was already attached to the opposite pillar. We had to hurry to get the chain across the gate in time, because car traffic into the cemetery—relatives bringing flowers to veterans' graves—was due to start at any moment.

May 30, 1946. Back then it was called Decoration Day, not Memorial Day. The temperature was already over eighty-five degrees at ten in the morning—rare for Upper Michigan any time of the year but especially unusual in the month of May. Sometimes we got snow in May.

A dandelion chain was a delicate piece of work and a thing of beauty. Putting one together was time consuming, and particularly so for the twelve-foot masterpiece Glenn and I had painstakingly assembled that morning. Each link was fashioned from a hollow dandelion stem, the smaller top end shoved into the bottom end, friction holding it together. It required careful handling; the chain could easily snap under its own weight.

We laid the chain on the ground and scampered into the cemetery where dandelions grew in profusion along the edges of the graves. Snatching several large flowers, we ran back to the gate, pinched off the blossoms, and made enough links to allow the chain to reach from one gatepost to the other. It hung across the gate like a cable on a suspension bridge.

The final touch was a shiny rectangle made from cigarette-package tinfoil. We fastened it to the center of the chain to resemble a metal lockbox from a distance. The dandelion chain stretched across the cemetery gate, glinting like polished brass in the morning sunlight, just like the real thing. The original cemetary gate had been removed many years ago, for whatever reason, and nobody would expect a chain across the entrance, certainly not on Decoration Day.

We finished just in time. A tan '36 Ford barreled down the hill toward the cemetery gate, tires furiously spitting out gravel stones in all directions.

Glenn and I dove into the tall tansy weeds by the cemetery gate. "It's Halapa an' his ol' lady," Glenn cackled. "He's inna real sweat t'drop off his flowers. This ought'a be good."

The Ford was doing about forty when—twenty yards from the cemetery gate—Arne Halapa saw the dandelion chain. He slammed on the brakes. The car skidded and spun, throwing gravel high into the air. Helmi Halapa, wide-eyed, straight-armed the dashboard, bracing herself.

Dust boiled up as the Ford slid to a stop a yard short of the gate. Halapa hopped out and inspected the dandelion chain. With one irate swipe he broke it and stomped back to the car.

"Whut wuz it?" his wife asked.

Arne let loose with a stream of ripe curses, many of which I'd never heard before. Tires chewed gravel as the car shot through the gate.

We emerged from the weeds. "You hear whut he said?" Glenn asked.

"I hope I kin remember all them words," I said.

As soon as Halapa's car pulled out of sight around the first curve in the cemetary, we jumped out of the weeds, made the necessary repairs on the chain, and restrung it across the gate.

Emil Hangas was next with his 1941 four-door Buick. During World War II no automobiles had been produced, and any '41 model was highly prized, even considered new. Emil loved his Buick—its fresh coat of Johnson's Wax gleamed in the morning sunlight as he approached the cemetary.

When Emil saw the dandelion chain, he stood on the brakes. The Buick fishtailed violently and screeched to a halt in front of our chain. Emil got out and peered at it up close, fingering it. He didn't snap the chain with his hands, though. He stomped back to his car and drove right through it. Our precious handiwork snagged on the Buick's front bumper and got dragged far into the cemetary.

Glenn and I sighed, got to our feet, and trudged up the hill toward town. Next week school would be out, and the dandelion-chain caper had been a warm-up for the many ambitious scientific projects we planned to tackle during the summer vacation.

"Whut'll we do now?" Glenn asked.

"I gotta swell idea for building a shotgun," I said.

I slipped the .410 shotgun shell into one end of a three-foot length of galvanized-iron water pipe. The shell slid in smoothly but only up to the flange on the end of the shell casing, the flange just wide enough to catch the lip of the pipe, as it should. The shell sat snugly just inside the end of the pipe.

"See? A perfect fit," I told Glenn. "All we gotta do is carve a stock, make a trigger, and hook it up to a firing pin, and we got us a shotgun." Glenn nodded eagerly. We were still a few years shy of being able to get hunting licenses, but building our own shotgun was an intoxicating prospect.

The two of us were in my grandfather's woodshed, amidst a collection of ancient tools scattered around on a worn wooden workbench. Eager to get started, I clamped the pipe in the workbench vice and began to file down the ragged edges on one lip of the pipe. A shotgun barrel of galvanized iron instead of tempered steel was a suicidal idea, but we didn't know that.

"Whut'll I do while yer filing th'pipe?" Glenn asked.

I pointed at a two-by-four. "You kin start carving a stock out of that."

Glenn looked over the rough-hewn length of wood, mentally calculating the effort involved in carving a shotgun stock from it. "I'll work on the barrel and *you* carve the stock."

I agreed and handed the file to Glenn. With my years of experience carving model airplanes from blocks of balsa wood, a shotgun stock was easy.

In the days that followed we made excellent progress. Glenn filed the edges of the water pipe and then vigorously applied steel wool until the pipe glowed with a lethal gun-metal luster of a honest-to-goodness gun barrel. With a spokeshave and wood chisel, I transformed the rough two-by-four into a realistic-looking shotgun stock. I was busily sanding the stock when my Uncle Arvid looked in the woodshed door.

"What're you guys making?"

"A shotgun," I said.

Arvid inspected the carved two-by-four, which actually *did* look like a gun stock. "That looks pretty good. What're ya gonna use for a barrel?"

Glenn proudly held up the gleaming water pipe. "This."

Arvid frowned. "Is that a water pipe?"

"Used to be," Glenn said. "It's a shotgun barrel now."

Something about our project disturbed Arvid. I couldn't imagine what it was, since we were doing such an excellent job.

"Gun barrels ain't iron," Arvid said. "A barrel made out of a water pipe will blow up."

"Aw, I don't think so," I said. "It's only gonna to be a little .410 shotgun, not a twelve gauge."

Not wanting to dampen our enthusiasm, Arvid didn't argue. "You figured out how to make a trigger mechanism yet?"

"Not yet," I said. "We'll probably do that tomorrow."

Arvid scratched his jaw and stared thoughtfully out the open door toward the woods. "How would you guys like a camp?"

"What'ja say?" I said with surprise. I must not have heard him right. I would have sworn that he'd said "How would you guys like a camp?"

Arvid repeated it. "A camp—how'd you guys like a camp?"

"You mean . . . a real camp out in the woods?"

"Yeah. Yer Uncle Arne and I built one about twenty years ago. We weren't much older than you two."

"Where is it?" Glenn asked.

"Not far. About a mile east of here."

"An' you're gonna let us use it?" I asked.

"You kin *have* it if you want it. Gonna take a lot of fixin' up, though, but you got lot'sa time this summer if you quit working on that shotgun."

"When kin we see the camp?" Glenn wanted to know.

"How about right now?"

Arvid claimed that we were following a trail, but I couldn't see it. If this was a trail, it was completely overgrown. Finally, after a half hour of plowing through ferns, poplar saplings, and sticker bushes, Arvid stopped. "Here it is."

I couldn't see a thing. "Where?"

Arvid pointed. "There."

Sure enough, beyond a wall of tangled trees and brush there was a dark mass. Glenn and I excitedly scrambled through the dense foliage and discovered a small log cabin. It was eight feet by eight feet, made from rough unchinked logs with large air gaps between them and a pine-board roof covered with ragged tar paper. A lone window had two of its four panes broken. The wooden door had long since fallen from its hinges and lay in the ferns. Porcupines had feasted on the door for years, and it looked like a half-eaten graham cracker.

At age thirteen I was only a little over five-feet tall but had to duck going through the low doorway. The inside was bare, except for a carpet of porcupine poop covering the splintery wooden floor.

"What a great camp!" I exclaimed.

"You bet!" Glenn chimed in.

Bright and early the next morning Glenn and I were prowling through the Republic town dump, looking for stuff for our new camp.

We were veritable experts on the dump, having spent most of our after-school hours there. We set dump fires, thus satisfying our adolescent lust for arson, and when the smoke and flames drove the rats out of hiding, we picked them off with our B-B guns. There was always plenty of neat things in the dump—all free, of course. We knew exactly where everything of value was, so that morning we didn't waste time rooting through piles of useless trash.

I snapped my fingers. "The '32 Plymouth!"

Glenn nodded. Nothing else had to be said. Flushing out irate rats, we scrambled through squashed cardboard boxes, tin cans, old newspapers, and smashed produce crates toward the wrecked car. From previous excursions in this sector of the dump, we knew the Plymouth had two very serviceable seat cushions which would make excellent camp beds.

Fortunately, the car's doors were missing, which made our job easier. We reached in, brushed the rat droppings off the cushions, and pulled the seats out. With great effort we dragged them up through the garbage we'd just navigated and plopped them down on the dump road.

"I guess we'll haf'ta make two trips," I said, trying to catch my breath.

Glenn shook his head. "Naw, takes too long. We just pile one on top of the other an' carry 'em both at once."

The trip involved plenty of sweat, much of it dripping on our prized seat cushions. We had to put down our load several times to hack away at the thick underbrush on the so-called trail to the camp. We'd brought along a couple of sickles for that very purpose.

The seat cushions occupied much of the camp floor space, but they definitely added a homey touch. We rushed back to the dump to get additional furniture. Glenn found a small table with only one leg missing. We ripped off one of the other legs, the plan being to nail one end of the table to the wall. It would work just fine. In the pile of trash from the Red Owl grocery store there was a perfectly good orange crate which, once nailed onto the log wall, would serve nicely as a cupboard. A wooden kitchen chair was missing its back, but it had four sturdy legs, so we took it.

When the camp was furnished, we began repairing the structure. Tree moss was plentiful, and we took huge handfuls and plugged up the gaps between the logs. There was no money to buy new tar paper, so we patched the roof with old tar paper scavenged from the dump. We located a few hinges and rehung the door, although there was plenty of open-air space around the edges where the porcupines had chewed through. We replaced the two broken window panes with cardboard.

A few days later the two of us revisited the dump on the off chance that someone might have made a valuable deposit since our last visit.

I pointed off to the left. "You see what I see?"

"What? Where?"

"Right next to that pile of rotten lettuce."

"My gawd," Glenn said in a hushed voice. "Is that whut I *think* it is?"

I didn't reply but headed down the slope, quickly tromping over the now-familiar mountains of trash. Glenn followed. We stopped in front of a potbellied stove.

It wasn't a big stove—only one lid on top—but it was perfect for the camp. And whoever had thrown the stove away had even been thoughtful enough to discard the stovepipe.

I reached down and reverently touched the stove. "Y'know what this means? Now we can cook!" Neither of us had ever cooked anything in our lives, but how difficult could it be?

"An' we kin go campin' in the winter an' won't freeze our butts off," Glenn added enthusiastically.

Charged with adrenaline, we each grabbed one end of the stove and began to muscle it up to the road. It was small but made of cast iron, and it felt like we were carrying a Buick. By the time we got it to the road we were panting like dogs and had to stop to catch our breath. Being typical pre-adolescent males, neither of us was about to admit that we weren't strong enough to carry this stove the mere mile out to the camp, so we sucked in one last gulp of air, picked up the stove, and started off.

Looking back on it, carrying that stove along the overgrown, twisting little trail through the woods was the most gawd-awful job I've ever undertaken. Every muscle in my body was screaming. Sweat streamed down my face, stinging my eyes. Large green-bellied flies landed on my nose and sat there, sopping up my perspiration as we stumbled along the path.

Finally, I couldn't stand it any longer and put my end of the stove down on the ground.

"I think I've got a hernia," I gasped.

Glenn quickly laid his end of the stove down. "Whut's a hernia?"

"I dunno, but my pa's got one, an' he don't lift anything heavy anymore."

It was a monumental struggle, but when we got to the camp, it was all worth it. The stove fit perfectly between the door and our only window, although we now had to climb over a car-seat bed in order to get in and out. Excited with our new acquisition, I cried, "Let's build a fire in it!"

"Ya think we ought'a go back an' get th'stove pipe first?" Glenn asked.

The time for the consummating act—spending a night in our very own camp—was now at hand. I was staying with my grandparents that summer while my mother and father were working in Milwaukee. My grandmother—a veteran lumber-camp cook when she was younger—was no stranger to living in the woods, and consequently she was an easy touch when I mentioned the overnight at the camp. She merely nodded her consent. My mother would've quickly vetoed the idea, convinced that I'd become lost and get eaten by bears.

Glenn and I filled two old burlap potato sacks with pillows, blankets, cooking and eating utensils, a candle, wooden matches, an axe, fishing tackle, and a can of live night crawlers. We omitted pajamas, knowing of course that serious campers slept in their underwear.

Another sack was filled with our idea of nutritious food—white bread, peanut butter, Velveeta cheese, catsup, bottles of creme soda, and two packages of Twinkies. We added a can of pork and beans, although it was totally unnecessary since there was a small stream close to the camp, and we had it in mind to catch a mess of trout for dinner.

We transported the overnight supplies to the camp with only a single minor mishap. The bait can had overturned in the potato sack, and the night crawlers had escaped, burrowing into my bedding. I retrieved the ones I could find and stuffed them back into the can.

Glenn grinned craftily as we began unpacking. "Wanna see whut I brought along?" He reached into his sack and pulled out an old blackened coffee pot and a small paper bag half filled with ground coffee. "I snuck 'em out of the house."

"Coffee! Great!" I exclaimed. This was going to be a night of wild debauchery.

"If we're gonna have trout for supper, we better go fishing," Glenn said.

We quickly stashed our groceries in the orange-crate cupboard, threw our bedding on the car seats, and began unsnarling the feisty backlashes in our Montgomery Ward fishing reels.

Something hit the roof with a loud splat. Then another. More in quick succession. Finally, a steady drumming.

It was raining.

Several sharp pings on the stove top let us know that our roof repairs may have been less than satisfactory. I jumped up from my car seat and placed one of our pans on the stove to catch the drip.

"There's one right over my bed here," Glenn said, rubbing a wet spot on the top of his head. I handed him the other pan.

Glenn had also brought along two coffee cups which were immediately pressed into service to catch other leaks. Finding still another leak over my bed, I placed the open coffee pot on my pillow.

The rain was really coming down now, and the leaks in the roof were too numerous to count. We tried jockeying our beds around on the floor to escape the drips, but there was no room to maneuver. It was coming down all over the inside of the cabin. In desperation we flung the empty potato sacks over the car seats in a futile attempt to sop up the rainwater.

"Firewood!" I cried. "We gotta get firewood before it gets all wet."

Both of us dashed outside into the downpour and frantically began snatching up dead twigs and pine branches from the ground. There was plenty of it around, but it was rapidly getting soaked. We carried in two huge armloads.

I was dripping wet and grabbed one of the burlap sacks from my bed and towelled off my head as best I could, impregnating my hair with the pungent fragrance of rotten potatoes.

The rain clouds had blotted out the afternoon light, and it was now quite dark in the camp. While Glenn emptied the rapidly filling pans and cups, I lit a candle, dripped a pool of wax onto the wooden table, and plunked the candle upright into the wax puddle.

Glenn ripped off his shirt and wrung it out into the puddles on the floor. "Jeez, it's cold in here. Let's light a fire."

I opened the little door on the stove and peered inside. Unfortunately, our stovepipe didn't have an elbow or rain deflector on the top end, so the rain was running directly down the inside of the pipe, creating a large puddle in the stove.

I grabbed one of the potato sacks from the bed and used it to soak up the water. Satisfied, I threw in handfuls of twigs and branches and put a lighted match to it. Nothing happened.

"We need some dry paper to get 'er going."

The only paper we had was the sack that held the ground coffee and one of my prized *Batman* comic books. The choice was simple. Glenn dumped the ground coffee into the coffee pot and placed the pot under our biggest leak, reasoning that the water-coffee mixture would be just about right when we were ready to brew up the coffee. I stuffed the empty paper sack in the stove and lit it.

That did the trick. The drier twigs burst into flame, and the larger branches began burning. Soon the fire was going good.

There was only one problem. The smoke wasn't going up the stovepipe; it was billowing into the room.

Glenn gave me an irritated look. "Don'cha know anything 'bout building a fire?"

I jerked a thumb at the smoking stove. "Yer so smart, *you* fix it."

The fact was, we were *both* experts at building fires, but only at the town dump.

Glenn peered inside the stove and then checked the damper on the stovepipe. Everything appeared to be in order except that we were getting smoked out. I opened the cabin door, and Glenn knocked the cardboard out of the window panes. Soon the air flowing in the window and out the open door helped clear the smoke a bit.

I sat down on a soggy car seat and wiped my burning eyes with a damp shirt sleeve. "Let's make supper. I'm gettin' hungry."

Since our fishing plans had gotten rained out, we decided on a menu of grilled cheese sandwiches, pork and beans, creme soda, and Twinkies. Toasting the sandwiches would normally have been simple by merely plopping them on the hot stove top and flipping them over a few times. But the leak directly above the stove presented a problem. To keep the sandwiches dry, Glenn held a pan above the stove top to catch the rainwater.

We'd forgotten to bring a spatula, so I used my hunting knife, carving the sandwiches loose from the hot stove top from time to time and then flipping them over with the knife blade. The fire was going really good now, so good, in fact, that the sandwiches were turning into charcoal bricks.

Both of us were hungry as wolves, and we elected to forego heating up the pork and beans. I ripped the can open with my knife (we had also forgotten a can opener), and we took turns eating the beans directly from the can. The charcoal flavor of the cheese sandwiches was toned down effectively with layers of catsup and peanut butter, and we washed the whole thing down with lukewarm creme soda. We sat back and burped contentedly after our splendid meal.

"Whaddaya say we make some coffee to go with the Twinkies?" Glenn suggested.

Neither of us had ever made coffee before, but that didn't slow us down one bit. I grabbed the coffee pot which held the half pound of ground coffee, totally muddied with the rainwater that had been dripping into it for the past few hours, and placed it on the hot stove.

In no time the pot of coffee was steaming and bubbling. Glenn bravely held out his cup.

"We don't have a coffee strainer," I said.

"Who needs a coffee strainer?" Glenn said. After all, we were Upper Michigan campers.

I began pouring coffee into Glenn's cup, but the coffee didn't actually pour. It tumbled out of the pot in large inky chunks.

Glenn peered into his cup and didn't make a move to drink it. He was waiting for me to try it first.

I filled my cup and experimentally sniffed. It *smelled* like coffee.

I took a tentative gulp. The lethally strong brew oozed down my throat like road tar. My heart began to pound erratically, and my stomach thought seriously about sending the coffee back up.

"I don't think I'll have any coffee right now," I said, putting the cup down. "Might keep me awake."

"Whut'll we do now?" Glenn asked. It was only six o'clock. The rain had let up a little, but it was still coming down steadily. I could only count fifteen leaks now.

The light was still gloomy, and we had less than one inch of candle left. "Might as well go to bed," I said.

We squirmed around on the wet car seats, searching for the driest spots, and then rolled up in the damp blankets. Something was crawling up my leg. I reached down and pulled out a night crawler that had escaped the earlier search.

The fire in the stove was dying, aided by the water running down the stovepipe. Drops hissed merrily on the embers and others clinked musically in the pans and cups on the floor.

We opened up a package of Twinkies and happily munched on them while laying on our soggy beds. Glenn and I looked at one another with smoke-reddened eyes and grinned.

Life couldn't possibly get any better than this.

The Big Trip

n attractive blonde flight attendant halted the drink cart next to my seat. "Sir, would you like a glass of wine with lunch?"

"No, thank you. I'll have coffee," I said. Even though Europeans think it's quite a civilized custom, I could never get used to the idea of drinking wine with lunch.

"We'll be serving coffee after the meal, sir."

"I'd like coffee *with* the meal, please."

The blonde looked at me like I was some kind of alien. "I'll pass your request on to the other flight attendant," she said stiffly and rolled the drink cart down the aisle.

We were cruising in bright afternoon sunlight, but it was already nighttime in London where the British Airways 747 had taken off several hours and four time zones ago. I sat back, trying to ignore the rock 'em, sock 'em, in-your-face kung-fu movie playing on the forward bulkhead screen. Gazing idly down at the Atlantic Ocean thirty-five thousand feet below, I knew that Newfoundland would soon be visible. I was familiar with the route.

Moments later the first officer came on the speaker system. "Ladies and gentlemen, the southern shore of Newfoundland can be seen from the right-hand side of the aircraft."

Sure enough, there it was. I had already made plans to visit Newfoundland the following year.

I'm a travel junkie. If two months go by and I'm not jumping on an airplane, I get very cranky and begin dragging out maps, looking for new horizons to conquer. My passport has become raggedy from dozens of customs stamps pounded into it over the years.

On this particular junket I'd visited England, France, Denmark, Norway, Sweden, Finland, Russia, and Estonia—most of them I'd seen now for a second or third time. I was tired. There had too many countries to absorb in one trip. Was that Viking museum in Oslo or Stockholm? I couldn't remember, maybe it was Copenhagen.

I wasn't always so casual about travel. Pressing the button on the armrest, I tilted the seat back, smiling, remembering the one trip whose every detail would be forever etched in my memory.

In 1939, receiving a letter was a big deal for us poor folks in the wilds of Upper Michigan. I had to stand on tiptoes to yank it from the mailbox, and then I raced for the house, my dog Teddy right at my heels, barking furiously.

"Wegottaletter! Wegottaletter!" I ran into the kitchen holding it high above my head.

The only mail of any consequence we ever received was an occasional Sears Roebuck or Montgomery Ward mail-order package, which in itself was cause for a minor celebration. Who was writing us a letter? Practically everyone we knew lived right there in the sleepy little iron-mining town of Ishpeming.

"Give me that," my mother said, snatching the letter away from me before I had a chance to rip it open.

"It's from my sister Martha in Republic," she said, looking at the return address. "Why in the world would she write?" She held the letter up to the light from the kitchen window as if that might yield a clue.

My father was working on his third cup of coffee of the morning, getting ready to hike the two miles out to his little potato farm on the edge of town. "Why don'cha open it up an' see what she has to say?"

My mother ignored the question, staring off into space and tapping the sealed letter in her open palm. "I wonder if it's about Mummu. Maybe she's sick. She really didn't look all that well the last time we saw her."

Once a year my maternal grandmother—everyone called her Mummu—managed to get a ride from the town of Republic to visit us. Just shy of sixty, she had the stamina of a race horse. It was hard to think of her ever being sick.

My father shrugged. "Las' time she was here, she looked okay t'me. Open up the letter."

My mother's voice ratcheted up. "That was over a *year* ago. Anything could have happened to her by now."

The old man finally grabbed the letter from her hand. "Well, fer cryin' out loud, let's read it an' find out." He began tearing open one end of the envelope.

"No!" my mother shrieked. "You'll tear the paper inside! Get a knife." With all the excitement, Teddy began barking again.

Since we rarely received letters, we didn't have a letter opener, so the old man got a paring knife from a drawer, carefully slit open the letter, and handed it back to my mother.

She slowly unfolded the pages and read it. "Martha and Hugo are driving to Ishpeming a week from Saturday to do some shopping. She says that if we want to go to Republic for a visit, they'll take us there and drive us back." Relieved at the absence of bad news, my mother turned to me. "Would you like to go to Republic to see your grandma and grandpa?"

"You bet! Is it far?" I sincerely hoped it was. We didn't own a car, and at age six I'd never been anywhere.

My mother shrugged and looked at the old man for help. "How far is it?"

"Oh . . . about twenty miles."

"Twenty miles!" I exclaimed. I had no concept of how far that was, but it sounded like a considerable distance.

I dashed out to tell my pal Kippy.

Kippy, who lived across the ore-train tracks from us, was at his kitchen table, munching on a catsup sandwich, the Depression snack of choice in our neighborhood.

"We're gonna go to Republic!"

"Where's Republic?"

"It's where my grandma and grandpa live. It's twenty miles away!"

Kippy gazed out the window, trying to visualize how far twenty miles was.

"An' we're gonna go in a *car*!" I added.

Kippy's family didn't own a car either, so that got his attention. "Holy smoke! Ya ever been in a car?"

"I don' think so."

"Is it a Ford or a Chevy?" Kippy asked. The vast majority of the cars in Ishpeming were either one or the other.

Flustered, I said, "I dunno." I bolted for home to get more information.

Esther, my fifteen-year-old sister, wasn't happy about the trip. "Can't I stay home?" she pleaded with my mother. At fifteen, going anywhere with parents was horrible punishment.

"What's the matter with you?" my mother said sternly. "How often do you think we get to go on a trip like this?"

"I can stay here and take care of the house," Esther offered.

My mother laughed at the radical suggestion. "Sure . . . and have you inviting your silly girlfriends over here to sit around and drink coffee." My mother felt that unless it was Christmas or some other high holiday, only responsible adults should be allowed to drink coffee. "You're going with us, the *both* of you, and that's final."

She didn't have to lay down the law to me. I was a travel junkie in the making.

My mother wrote back to Aunt Martha and accepted the invitation. From then on our house was a tornado of activity. A mountain of paraphernalia—classified as essential trip baggage—began to take shape in a corner of the kitchen, and it continued to grow as the days passed. Blankets, sweaters, and galoshes were brought out. It was July, but this was Upper Michigan, and no one ever trusted the weather. Sloan's Liniment and a hot-water bottle were added for roadside medical emergencies. On a journey of this length, food was vitally important, too. Everyone added their favorites: soda crackers, peanut butter, fig bars, Cracker Jacks, canned kippered herring, French's mustard, and plenty of Elson's soda pop. My mother rummaged around in everyone's dresser drawers to find underwear without holes, because you never knew when you might get stranded in a strange place overnight. Esther resigned herself to going and tossed her swim suit onto the heap of stuff. My contribution was several cast-iron toy cars and a sand-box shovel, because I was sure I'd find a sandpile in Republic.

The old man casually mentioned that when we got to Republic

maybe Vahri, my grandfather, would take me fishing out at Pump House Lake. My only exposure to fishing had been leafing through my father's issues of *Field and Stream*. I'd drooled over pictures of grinning anglers in gleaming white boats, pulling up snarling northern pike as big as telephone poles.

"Fishing? I don' have a fishing pole!" I wailed. "How can I catch fish without a pole?"

The old man led me out to the woodshed—his answer to Fibber McGee's closet—where he somehow managed to locate a few fishhooks, a handful of split lead sinkers, a bobber cork, fishing line thick enough to beach a white shark, and a rusty old pole without a reel.

On Saturday morning, the day of the big trip, it was still dark when my mother stoked up the wood stove in the kitchen for some serious baking. On her yearly visits my grandmother always brought us two loaves of freshly baked Finnish coffee bread as a gift. My mother was convinced that she could outbake Mummu, so she was launching a full-scale Finnish-coffee-bread war, escalating it by taking *four* loaves to Republic.

When the bread was out of the oven my mother put her hair up in curlers and then woke my sister and put *her* hair in curlers. For lunch on the road, she made Spam sandwiches and a bowl of potato salad.

At ten o'clock I was standing in the middle of the street, acting as lookout. The Ishpeming water truck hadn't sprayed down the street yet, and as soon as I spotted a large cloud of dust, I ran into the house.

"THEY'RE COMIN'!"

Several of the neighbor men came out to look at Uncle Hugo's

'37 Ford. It was two years old but still pretty new by Ishpeming standards. Hugo obligingly opened the hood and showed off the powerful 60 horsepower V-8 engine.

The car was half filled with Aunt Martha's groceries—including a large watermelon—but we proceeded to cram in even more. All six of us climbed in the car, over and between the shopping bags and cardboard boxes. It was a dicey operation. My mother and Aunt Martha fought their way into the back seat and wedged my sister between them. I scrambled into the front seat, between Uncle Hugo and the old man, my short legs straddling the floor-mounted gearshift. Everyone except the driver had their laps full. I was in charge of the shopping bag full of clean underwear.

When we were finally packed into the car, like Barnum and Bailey circus clowns, Hugo turned on the ignition. The V-8 engine roared to life, and the Ford lumbered down the street, swaying precariously from side to side under the tremendous load. We were on our way.

The winding road to Republic was all gravel. It hadn't been graded in awhile, and the car bounced crazily over the washboard surface. Rocks thundered on the Ford's underbelly.

"Slow down!" Martha yelled at Hugo. "You wanna get us all killed?"

Hugo whipped his head around and yelled back, "I'm only goin' forty! Whaddaya want?"

Martha leaned forward and shouted in his ear. "I don't want to get in a car wreck! The last thing I need is to see my age printed in the newspaper!"

Forty miles an hour—holy smoke! I had no idea that car travel would be so exciting.

The thick, swirling road dust forced us to keep the windows up. The temperature inside the little Ford mounted; the heat was brewing a tart, pungent fragrance of warm Finnish coffee bread, Spam, and sweat.

"Why don't we sing a song?" my mother suggested.

Everyone launched into "You Are My Sunshine," the only song to which we all knew the words.

I was carefully watching every move Hugo made: jerking the steering wheel from side to side, alternately pushing the three floor pedals, and reaching across my leg to move the gearshift into different positions. By the time we reached Republic I knew I'd have it all down pat.

Hordes of bugs were committing suicide on the windshield, mixing with road film to create a greenish-brown paste. Hugo turned on the wipers, but it only stirred the mess around. Finally, he rolled down the window, and with his left arm extended he attempted to clean the windshield with a bandanna.

He was concentrating on this when we rounded a curve and came upon a series of deep potholes. Hugo quickly wrenched the wheel to one side but too late. The car plunged into one of the holes with a spring-bottoming jolt. The right front tire blew. In the back seat the big watermelon popped out of my sister's lap and fell on the floor. Esther moaned as she saw the split watermelon bleeding all over her shoes.

The Ford wobbled to a halt, and Hugo shut off the ignition. "Okay, everybody out."

Stepping on cardboard boxes, grocery bags, and each other, we piled out of the car and inspected the flat tire.

"Don't worry," Martha assured us. "This happens all the time. It shouldn't take long to put on the spare."

"The spare's at home," Hugo muttered, opening the trunk.

Martha couldn't believe it. "You left the spare tire at home? Why did you do a dumb thing like that?"

"I knew there wasn't gonna be enough room for the tire and all this stuff, so I left the spare. Don't worry, I'll patch the tube." Hugo pulled everything out of the trunk and put the stuff on the road to get at the tire tools. He then loosened the lugs on the wheel, placed the jack under the bumper, and began pumping. The Ford teetered dangerously as the corner of the car rose off the gravel.

In those days flat tires were a common headache on any automobile trip, but to me the flat was another thrilling episode of our adventure. I was thoroughly enjoying myself, although everyone else, for some reason, seemed to be a bit down in the mouth.

My mother attempted to inject some cheer into the group. "Let's have a picnic." Digging around in our belongings now sitting on the roadway, she magically produced a blanket, food and drink, forks, and a stack of plates. I was assigned to go into the adjacent field and tromp down tansy weeds to form a clearing. This proved to be a tough job since the seven-foot weeds had stalks as thick as my wrists.

While Hugo repaired the tire, the rest of us picnicked among the trampled tansies. The broken watermelon was still edible, so my mother salvaged it, slicing it up with a long kitchen knife. Each of us got a piece on a plate along with a Spam sandwich and a large dollop of potato salad.

The simmering midday sun beat down as we sat, kneecap to kneecap, around the blanket. Screeching crickets rudely informed us that we had no business being there. The rest of the insect world had more severe punishment in store. Flies and gnats of all descriptions zoomed out of the woods and gleefully zeroed in. They flew up our noses, into our ears, and got a free ride into our mouths on the food. To strengthen our solidarity, my mother led us in another round of "You Are My Sunshine."

After nearly an hour Hugo finally had a patch on the inner tube. He pumped it up and held it to his cheek, making sure that there were no other leaks. The tire was quickly reassembled and put back onto the wheel. I was crammed behind the gearshift again, and we were once more on our way.

During the picnic I'd glugged down two bottles of Elson's cream soda, and the washboard road was now seriously jiggling them around in my body.

"Ma, I gotta go to the toilet."

My mother rolled her eyes. "Do you have to poop?" The only thing she hadn't thought to bring was toilet paper.

"No."

Hugo brought the car to a halt. My father got out, took my arm, and pointed toward the woods. "Go," he said.

Many times, during a fierce cap-gun battle in the alleys of Ishpeming, my pals and I would think nothing of taking a leak behind a garbage can rather than stop the hostilities to go home and use the bathroom. But I'd never done it in the woods. I'd never *been* in the woods. It looked scary.

My sister began scrambling out of the back seat. "I gotta go, too."

"Which way are you going?" I asked.

"Which way are *you* going?"

"There," I said, pointing toward what appeared to be the least-menacing group of trees. "You gonna come with me?" I asked hopefully.

"Are you some kind of lame brain? I'm going over there." She pointed off in the opposite direction across the road.

Apprehensive, I ventured into the woods, every few steps glancing back toward the car. My mother was scowling through the car window. She wanted me out of sight while I did what I had to do, so I kept moving.

Trees closed around like a thick cloak. Now, all of the stupid crickets were quiet as mice. I could hear my heart thumping wildly. This was an evil place.

I did my business, zipped up my corduroy knickers, and headed back toward the car. Twigs snapped behind me, like footsteps. It couldn't be Esther, I thought; she went across the road. The snapping got closer. *It wasn't footsteps, it was pawsteps*!

I took off at a dead run, low-lying tree limbs slapping my face and ferns clutching at my ankles. I finally broke out into the open near the car and scrambled across the old man's knees, settling into my cozy niche between the two men. My sister was already in back, cool, calm, and collected. She obviously had never met a bear in the woods.

When we arrived at my grandparents' little white house on the edge of Republic, it was time for afternoon coffee. The Finnish custom of coffee and pastries was always strictly observed no matter how many visitors were present. Mummu dealt out place settings for eight on the little kitchen table sized to seat four. My mother flamboyantly produced her four loaves of coffee bread. My grandmother inspected them critically and said nothing. Coffee was poured for the grownups, but Esther and I had to drink Postum, a punchless, caffeine-free beverage that was popular at the time.

Before Vahri, my grandfather, could finish his third cup of coffee I was pestering him to take me fishing.

"First, you gotta get worms," Vahri said in his thick Finnish accent.

I'd forgotten about bait. "Where do we get worms?"

"By the pig pen."

"You have a pig?"

"Sure." He got up from the table and led me into the back yard. There, inside a split-log wooden pen, was a very large, very ugly, and very dirty pig.

I'd never seen a real live pig, and I crept up close to the side of the pen to get a good look. The pig scowled at me and emitted a threatening grunt.

"Don' get too close," Vahri warned. "He don' like kids.

Though, maybe he *would* like kids. He ain't ever tried one." Vahri chuckled at his own joke.

While I kept an eye on the pig, my grandfather dug for worms. It wasn't a hard job. A spadeful of dirt by the pigpen proved that worms did indeed like to cozy up to pigs, and in no time at all our bait can was filled with fat wigglers. I pulled my fishing gear from the car. Vahri showed me how to attach the metal leader, lead sinkers, the bobbing cork, and the hook to the fish line. That done, the two of us took off for Pump House Lake on my very first fishing adventure.

I'd had plenty of experience playing with worms in my sandpile at home, but putting one on a fish hook was a different story entirely.

Holding an squirming worm between my fingers, I looked to my grandfather for help.

"You gotta do it yourself," Vahri said. "How else you gonna learn? Anyway, I don' like to touch worms."

Ten minutes later, after a great deal of thrashing about which involved puncturing my thumb twice, I managed to get the worm on the hook.

I threw the line into the water. In a matter of seconds the end of the pole twitched and the cork bobber dipped in the water.

"I gotta bite!"

I yanked the line out of the water with such ferocity that the hook, sinker, and cork whipped over my head and landed in a clump of sticker bushes behind me. The hook was bare.

"No, no," Vahri advised patiently. "Give the fish a chance to eat the worm. An' don't holler like that. It scares the fish. It scares me, too."

But whatever was in that lake didn't scare easily. On my second attempt the pole jerked again, now more violently. The cork bobber completely disappeared from sight. This time I mightily resisted the impulse to yank the hook out of the water. The line jitterbugged around through the water, and the end of the pole bounced up and down.

Forgetting all about scaring the fish I yelled, "Whadda I do?"

"I think you bring 'im up now," Vahri said.

I hauled back on the pole. A thrashing fish burst out of the water, sparkling in the sunlight.

I hopped up and down, watching the fish flopping around on the rocky shore as Vahri removed the hook.

"Is it a northern pike?" I asked. I couldn't be sure. This fish wasn't quite as large as those *Field and Stream* northern pike I'd seen. It was five inches long.

"It's a perch," Vahri said, taking it off the hook.

Pike or perch, it couldn't spoil the moment. I'd caught my first fish, singlehandedly outsmarting it. I would learn on later fishing trips that Pump House Lake perch would bite on anything, including the red cellophane from Lucky Strike packages.

Hours later, we were headed back to Ishpeming. The Ford's gearshift knob drummed gently against my leg, and the low evening sun flickering through the trees on my face was producing a drowsy stupor. The most exciting day of my life was coming to an end, and there was nothing to be done about it. I was feeling sad.

"Ya ever drive a car?" Hugo asked me.

"No," I said, immediately on the alert.

"Wanna take over for awhile? I'm gettin' a li'l sleepy."

"Hugo, don't fool around now," Martha said sharply.

Hugo reached over and, without slowing the car, snatched me up with one hand, put me on his lap, and placed my hands on the steering wheel as he took his own completely off.

The car immediately veered off to the left. I swung the wheel way over to the right, heading the car toward the ditch. Hugo nudged the wheel with a finger and got us back on course.

"Hugo, be careful," my mother said from the backseat. My sister giggled. The old man suppressed a grin.

Hugo began making snoring sounds.

"Hugo, quit that!" Martha yelled.

He snored louder.

Let him sleep, I thought. I clutched the steering wheel tightly, moving it back and forth, getting the hang of it.

I felt a tap on my shoulder.

"Sir, you'll have to bring your seat into the upright position," the British Airways attendant was saying. "We're descending in preparation for landing at John F. Kennedy Airport."

My hands were still clutching the '37 Ford's steering wheel.

The smiling attendant offered me a steaming towel. "Where did you go during your stay in Europe?"

I told her about the multi-nation journey while I scrubbed my face and hands with the towel.

"Oh, my," she said with a smile. "All those countries. That must have been the most exciting trip you've ever taken."

I had to grin. "No, it wasn't. Not by a long shot."

The Tooth-Fairy Contract

My father picked me up and set me down on the edge of the kitchen table. "Open up an' lemme take a look in there."

I knew exactly what was in store; once the old man took me into the kitchen—his operating room—and put me up on the table, the die was cast. No turning back. No negotiations. No pleas for mercy. I fearfully opened my mouth.

"Put yer finger on it so I kin see which one is loose," he said.

I put a finger on the tooth and wiggled it. "Ith tha un."

He stared into my mouth for a second and then quickly reached in with his thumb and forefinger and yanked the tooth out. The old man inspected the tooth proudly. He loved pulling teeth because it saved money that otherwise would have gone into the dentist's pocket.

"Rub yer tongue over the hole. Did I get the right one?"

I rolled my tongue across the bleeding crater in my mouth and nodded.

"Okay, get down and spit in the sink," he said.

I spat blood into the kitchen sink and quickly ran the water so I wouldn't have to look at it. The old man had already yanked quite a few baby teeth out of my mouth, but I still couldn't stand the sight of my own blood.

My mother pulled out a tray of homemade ice cream from the refrigerator freezer. "Sit down at the table, and I'll give you a dish of vanilla."

Ice cream was my standard reward for allowing the old man to practice unanesthetized dentistry on me. Actually, ice cream *was* the anesthetic. I'd jockey a glob of ice cream into the bloody hole, and the cold numbed the pain. I was beginning to think that there were four flavors of ice cream: vanilla, chocolate, strawberry, and blood.

The old man handed me the tiny tooth. "Don't forget to put it under yer pillow."

Following each extraction I'd wrap the tooth in toilet paper and carefully place it under my pillow. The next morning I'd find a nickel in its place, left there by the tooth fairy. I could never figure out how that fairy could get the tooth out from underneath my pillow and put a nickel in there without me waking up. That was one sneaky tooth fairy.

That night I put the newly pulled tooth under my pillow, lay back, and waited. This time I was going to stay awake and catch the tooth fairy redhanded. Tact was necessary, though. I couldn't get the fairy mad because the nickels were certainly coming in handy, but I was curious to see who I was dealing with here. Was this a girl fairy or a boy fairy?

I didn't last an hour. My mother shook me awake the next morning, and under the pillow was a shiny, new buffalo-head nickel. The tooth fairy had struck again.

A week later I had another tooth problem—this time a toothache. At first I kept it to myself because the old man would surely have jerked out the offending tooth in a heartbeat, and I wasn't ready for another one of his extractions quite so soon. But the toothache kept getting worse, and I finally had to break down and tell him.

He grinned broadly, cracking his knuckles in anticipation. "Open up an' show me which one."

I stuck my finger way back in my wide-open mouth and touched the aching tooth. "Ith wun."

The old man put his finger in and tried to wiggle the tooth. "It ain't loose."

Now my mother got interested. "Let *me* take a look at it."

I opened my mouth again and pointed to the tooth.

She stared in and shook her head. "It's a molar, and it looks like a big cavity. We're going to have to take you to the dentist."

"Dentist?" my father cried. "Dentists cost money." He rolled up his sleeves and wrapped one arm around my head to hold me still. "Lemme jus' get a hold of that tooth again an'. . ."

"He's going to the dentist, and that's final," my mother declared.

On the periphery of my limited knowledge I'd heard about dentists, but I'd never actually been to one, so my information was sketchy. I trotted across the railroad tracks over to my pal Kippy's house. He was eight months older and knew a lot of things.

"Ya ever been to a dentist?" I asked Kippy.

Kippy grimaced in pain at the very mention of the word. "One time my ma took me. The dentist pulled out one a my teeth."

"That's nuthin.' My pa does that alla time."

"Yeah, but the dentist used some kind'a pliers."

"Pliers . . . to pull a tooth?" The thought sent shivers down my spine.

"Not only that, before he pulled the tooth he stuck a needle in my mouth, right where the tooth was."

"A needle? C'mon, y'mean with thread on it?"

"Nah. A big, hollow needle, long as a ruler. Stuck me good an' it hurt bad. The needle squirted some stuff in there, an' after awhile the tooth got numb."

"So it didn't hurt when he pulled the tooth out, right?" I asked hopefully.

"Sure, it hurt. Wusn't *that* numb. Lemme tell ya sumthin', don't ever go to a dentist. Ya won't like it."

The office of Dr. Otto Cruelle on Main Street in Ishpeming was only three blocks from our house, but it must have seemed a lot further to my father since he was carrying me, kicking and squirming, under his arm all the way. We went up a flight of stairs to the dentist's office where I was unceremoniously plunked down on a chair in the waiting room. The old man, breathing hard, kept a firm grip on my arm, knowing that if I got loose, he'd never catch me.

"I gotta go home an' pee," I pleaded with him.

"Ya did that before we left th'house. Jus' take it easy. The dentist's only gonna take a look at yer tooth."

Sure, I thought. He'll take one look at it and then haul out his long needle and pliers, and that will be the end of me.

The door leading to the inner room was closed, but it didn't effectively muffle the sounds coming from within. Some poor devil was crying out in pain, and it seemed as though it might have become a full-fledged scream had not someone been holding his jaw. The sounds finally diminished into pitiful whimpers and then silence.

After awhile the inner door opened, and a large man, ashen-faced, eyes glazed with pain, stumbled out. Without a word he opened the outer door to leave. I surged forward to bolt out directly behind him, but the old man was too quick for me and grabbed the back of my pants.

Dr. Cruelle came out and grinned broadly at me with large, tobacco-stained teeth. The front of his white smock was liberally peppered with drops of fresh blood.

"Well, hello there, young fella. C'mon in and have a seat."

The old man lifted me bodily from the chair and frogmarched me into Cruelle's inner office.

It was a spooky room. What resembled a barber's chair was surrounded by various instruments of torture. Since Kippy had provided detailed information, I already knew what most of them were. An assortment of lethal knives, picks, and pliers were laid out on a tray next to the chair. The silver pencil-like device at the end of two long arms with wires and pulleys was an electric drill for cutting through your teeth down to the nerves. The big porcelain bowl on the opposite side of the chair was for spitting out the blood after the tools had done their grisly job. To convince patients that all of this was necessary, a large chart on one wall had pictures—in living color—of teeth and gums in various stages of ugly rot and disease.

I twisted in my old man's grasp in one last-ditch effort to make a break for it, but he held me fast.

Dr. Cruelle patted the seat of the leather chair. "Okay, young fella, why don't you hop up here, and we'll take a look at that tooth."

"Y'know what?" I said brightly. "It don't ache at all any more. I might as well go home."

My old man picked me up and put me in the chair.

Dr. Cruelle positioned a long-necked lamp, switched it on, and directed the light onto my face. He leaned over me with a big, insincere smile. I could smell stale cigars on his hot breath. "Now be a brave boy and open your mouth so I can take a look."

I opened up. Cruelle immediately produced a long, sharp pick that he'd been craftily hiding behind his back and swiftly and expertly stuck it in my mouth. Instantly, there was a sharp pain in my tooth.

Cruelle stopped smiling and nodded. "Uh-huh. Well, you've got a pretty big cavity in that tooth." He turned to my father. "It's a baby molar, and it won't come out by itself for about five years. But it's too far gone. It'll have to come out now."

"How much will it cost?" my father asked.

"Five dollars."

The old man twitched with shock. I quickly volunteered my opinion. "Five bucks? Boy, that's a lot! Too much, huh?"

My father nodded. "Well, yeah, but I guess we gotta do 'er. When kin ya pull it?" he asked the dentist.

"I can do it right now."

I went rigid with fear. The old man placed a heavy hand on my shoulder, pinning me to the chair.

Dr. Cruelle flashed another phony smile as he shuffled his bloodletting instruments around on the tray. "Don't worry, it'll all be over before you know it. And you know what I'll do before I take out the tooth? I'll give you a tiny little shot of novocaine—which you won't feel at all—and then the tooth will be nice and numb."

That was pure baloney. Kippy had warned me about the pain from the needle.

"I don' want no shot."

Dr. Cruelle had his back to me. When he turned around he was concealing something. "Don't want the novocaine? My, what a brave young man you are. But I think you better have it. Now, why don't you open your mouth again."

I just sat there with my mouth clamped shut, but the old man tightened his grip on me. "Open up."

I obeyed. Cruelle leaned over me and brought his hand up to my mouth. He was trying to hide the needle, but I could see it anyway. It was bigger than Kippy had said—two-feet long, thick as a railroad spike—and it was going into my mouth.

Cruelle slipped his little finger into the corner of my mouth and pulled my cheek back to insert the needle.

All of my front teeth were permanent, strong and sharp. I'd put a lot of rigorous miles on them, cutting through rock-hard candy canes and jawbreakers. I bit down hard on Cruelle's finger and hung on.

"Arrgghh! ##@@*!!" Cruelle yelled. I chomped down even harder.

My father didn't know what was happening, thinking perhaps that Cruelle was having trouble getting the needle in my gum.

Cruelle turned wide-eyed to him. "Tell that little @#%**!! to let go of my finger!"

The old man put a half-nelson on me, and I finally let loose.

The dentist stared down at his stricken finger, then shook his fist at me. "Get him out of here!"

On the way home I expected the old man to give me a swat or two across the head, but not so. He was relieved that the dentist had gotten so mad when I bit him that he forgot to charge us for the aborted tooth extraction.

"Y'know, yer gonna have to get that tooth yanked out anyhow," he said.

"I ain't going back there an' have him stick me with that big needle."

"Th'tooth ain't loose enough fer me to pull it."

"That's okay, I'll keep it then."

"Don't forget, the tooth fairy'll give ya a nickel fer it," the old man added.

"I ain't goin' back for no lousy nickel."

He thought about that and then said, "Whaddaya figure the tooth fairy would haf'ta pay ya to go back to the dentist?"

"The tooth fairy ain't got that kind'a money."

"Well, maybe the fairy'd getcha one a them little cars ya like so much."

The old man really knew my weaknesses. I had a great fondness for little cast-iron toy cars and trucks. My backyard sandpile was a vast network of roads that these cars and trucks—with the help of my hand and my shouting, "varroom, varroom, varroom"—travelled up and down every day. Unfortunately, my current inventory of vehicles was in sad shape and in need of replacement. Most were missing at least one wheel, and the paint had long since been blasted off by the many miles through the sand.

The old man added, "Maybe we ought'a go over to Newberry's an' look at some a those cars."

I had to stand on tiptoes to look at the fleet of toy cars on the countertop in Newberry's. Aligned in orderly rows were tiny sedans, yellow taxicabs, ambulances, gasoline trucks with a flying red horse logo, black and white police cars, dump trucks, and streamlined Greyhound buses with silver windows.

I'd checked them all out before. Often, in fact. On Saturday afternoons Kippy and I would journey down to Newberry's to admire the cast-iron toys. However, at twenty-five cents apiece all we could do was look.

"See anything ya like?" the old man asked.

"Yeah, but nuthin' worth goin' to the dentist for."

We turned away to leave, but my eyes happened to fall on a stack of small boxes piled on the adjoining counter. Plastered on each box in big bold red letters was:

SPEEDO MODELS
SMOKE-EATER FIRE ENGINE
1/40 scale, complete in every detail!

I grabbed one of the boxes and peered through the cellophane window, then quickly opened one end and pulled out the model. The fire engine was too big to hold safely in my hand, so I placed it on the floor.

It was eight inches long, considerably larger than the other toy cars. The ceiling lights in Newberry's reflected off the mirror-like red paint on the long hood. A gleaming silver siren was attached to the cab roof. Removable white ladders were mounted by tiny metal hooks on each side of the chassis. It had glass windows, something you didn't see in toy cars in those days. I experimentally pushed the model across the floor. It rolled silently on authentic-looking, black rubber tires.

The old man, recognizing quality when he saw it, eyed the fire engine suspiciously. "How much does that cost?"

I glanced down at the price sticker on the box. "A dollar."

His mouth fell open. "A dollar? A dollar? Fer a toy truck?"

"Yeah, but it's the best one I've ever seen." It really was, and I had to have it. I thought long and hard before adding, "If the tooth fairy will bring me this fire engine, I'll let the dentist pull my tooth."

Dr. Cruelle played it safe this time and wore heavy-duty rubber gloves. One of the rubber fingers bulged with a bandage underneath. The dentist looked at me warily as he arranged his equipment on the chair-side tray. "We're not going to have any more trouble with you, are we?"

"Nope."

"No more biting?"

"No, sir. We're gonna make a deal with the tooth fairy."

Cruelle looked questioningly at my father. "A deal with the tooth fairy?"

The old man replied sadly, "That's right. The fairy's gonna haf'ta shell out a bundle to get this tooth."

Cruelle obviously didn't put a lot of stock in deals with tooth fairies because the first thing he did was to stuff a large wad of cotton in my mouth to prevent me from biting down. Then he quickly positioned the needle and injected the novocaine. It hurt, but not as bad as I thought it would.

Fifteen minutes later it was all over, and we were trudging home. My jaw was stiff and numb, and there was a wad of cotton gauze in my mouth to soak up the blood. But I had survived. The tooth was in my hand, and I clung onto it like it was the Hope diamond.

"How will the tooth fairy know that I want that fire engine?" I asked the old man.

"Them fairies know all that stuff," he said.

I stopped and went over to the curb on Main Street to spit out more blood. "I hope so. I don't want to wake up tomorrow morning and find a lousy nickel under the pillow."

As soon as my eyes opened, I was wide awake. I carefully lifted my head, turned over, and propped myself up on my elbows. I raised the pillow.

Nothing. Not even a nickel.

I jumped out of bed and struggled into my clothes, ready to run downstairs to tell the old man what I thought of tooth fairies.

But there it was, on top of the dresser. The little white ladders and the windshield glass glowing softly in the early-morning light filtering through the bedroom window. A note was resting against the red chassis.

YOUR HARD HEAD WOULD HAVE DENTED THIS
IF I'D PUT IN UNDER THE PILLOW.
THE TOOTH FAIRY
P.S. FROM NOW ON IT'S BACK TO NICKELS.

The handwriting bore an uncanny resemblance to that of my father's, but it was probably just a coincidence.

The Blizzard of '38

inter blizzards are common here in Upper Michigan, but on Monday, January 24, 1938, we had the granddaddy of all blizzards. I wasn't quite five years old at the time, but I still remember the Blizzard of '38.

"Hurry up, Ma. The snow's gonna melt!"

My mother was struggling to untwist the suspenders that held up my knickers. She pulled back her hand as if to give me a swat, which was the standard signal between the two of us that I'd better keep quiet. "It's not going to melt. Now stand still, or you'll never get outside."

With her experience getting me dressed to play in the snow, my mother could have easily suited up medieval knights in armor. I had plenty of armor, too: long underwear, thick woolen socks that climbed up my thighs, two heavy shirts, corduroy knickers, a sweater, a six-foot muffler, and a thick woolen snowsuit. Boots, three sizes too big, allowed air to circulate around my feet. Fully clothed I weighed in at about two hundred pounds. If I ever fell down, I never would've gotten back up.

This ritual took place every day during the long winter. My mother would spend a half hour dressing me to go outside and another half hour stripping off the layers when I came back in. Today she was in a particularly hostile mood because she was interrupting her Monday-morning washing to suit me up.

She pulled the sweater over my already bulging torso. "Next winter you're going to do this all by yourself."

The final step—the trickiest—was inserting me and my three cubic yards of clothing into the snowsuit. This operation was the equivalent of stuffing a barrage balloon into an inner tube. Grunting with exertion, my mother tugged the snowsuit over my corduroy knickers, zipped me into it, and coiled the muffler around my neck twelve times and finally across my nose.

I lurched toward the kitchen door, the air whooshing out of the oversized arctics as I carefully put one foot down in front of the other.

I stopped. "Ma, I gotta pee," I murmured through the thick muffler.

She had already gone back to feeding underwear through the Maytag wringer. "If I have to take that snowsuit off so you can pee, I'm not putting it back on again. You decide what you're going to do."

I was mentally debating the pros and cons of this when my father came in, carrying wash in from the clothesline. The clothes were frozen into odd-shaped planks.

"I better get the rest of that wash off the line," the old man said as he stood two pairs of long underwear up against the kitchen wall. "It's startin' t'snow an' blow pretty good."

Realizing I might be pressed for playtime, I decided against the pee. "I think I'll go out now."

My father shook his head. "No, you're stayin' in. The weather's gettin' too bad."

My mother began to unwind the muffler from around my neck.

"But I wanna go sleigh riding," I wailed.

"There'll be plenty of snow fer sleigh ridin' after this storm," the old man said.

He didn't know how good a prediction that was.

By four o'clock it was totally dark. The heavy snow lashing in from the north completely eclipsed the bright street light next to our house. Our old wooden shack shuddered with every wind blast, causing the storm windows to rattle like machine guns. Bursts of cold air rocketed in along the edges of the windows.

My favorite winter pastime was listening to our floor-model Zenith radio. I'd get down on the rug, cozying up beside the radio to draw heat from the glowing tubes in the large wooden cabinet. But this afternoon, after twiddling the tuning dial all the way around, I could only pick up static.

The frozen hinges on our outside storm door squawked, and someone rapped on the kitchen door. My mother opened it.

We gawked at the short, squatty snowman with moving eyes. The creature clumped into the kitchen and slowly unwound a snow-caked muffler from its head.

Bertha Maki's plump face peered out.

My mother recovered quickly. "Bertha, my goodness. With this weather we didn't expect company tonight."

Bertha stomped the snow from her boots onto the kitchen linoleum. "Oh, I just thought I'd stop over and say hello."

Bertha never stopped by just to say hello. She was tuned in to every piece of juicy gossip in the city of Ishpeming and felt it her civic duty to pass the choicest transgressions on to the public. She knew exactly how many Italians were still making bootleg wine on

Superior Street. She had predicted to the day when the Lutheran minister's son would start playing hanky-panky with Eugenia Bergstrahl, the daughter of one of our most upstanding Sunday-school teachers. Bertha knew the precise net worth of everybody in Ishpeming and could tell you if some family who was buying a new refrigerator would be able to make the payments. Neither blizzard nor gloom of night would stay Bertha Maki from the swift completion of her appointed muckraking rounds.

Bertha shed her heavy coat and handed it to my mother. She sat down at the kitchen table, smacking her lips in anticipation of launching into her latest exposè. "I happened to be going by Tilly Niemi's this morning, and you'd never know she was a widow from looking at her wash line. A pair of long johns hangin' there—too big to be hers, that's for sure. She didn't leave 'em out there too long, 'cause I came by later and they were gone. Pulled 'em down real quick before she thought anybody noticed." Bertha chuckled with the knowledge that she'd once again ferreted out a steamy indiscretion.

My mother, anticipating a more-detailed accounting of Tilly Niemi's sins from Bertha, pointed at me and then the stairs. "Go up to your room."

"But Ma, I ain't had supper yet, and Bertha ain't finished her story either."

"It's not an Uncle Remus story. I'll call you when supper's ready."

I went upstairs and got down next to the floor register in my bedroom. Floor registers were quite effective for allowing heat to flow to the upstairs bedrooms, but they were even better as listening devices. I listened closely, but Bertha's story must have had a real spicy ending because she began speaking Finn, a language I'd heard a lot but still couldn't understand.

When I came down for supper Bertha was gone. The old man had convinced her that with the worsening storm she should get home while she could still make it. The last person in the world he wanted to get snowed in with was Bertha Maki.

My mother filled everyone's plates, and we dug into our usual Monday-evening fare, hash made from Sunday's roast beef and boiled potatoes and anything else that my mother felt inclined to throw into it.

"Th'radio ain't working," I grumbled. "We can't hear Fibber McGee, Henry Aldrich, or nuthin'."

My sister, Esther, wasn't too happy either. The blizzard was threatening her high-school social calendar. "I'm supposed to go to glee club tonight," she complained.

After supper my father got up from the table and went into the little storm porch off the kitchen. He pried open the outside door, looked out, and returned, shaking his head. "Y'can't see yer hand in front of yer face out there. An' my back sez it's gonna be a dandy." Using the pain in his back as a gauge, the old man could forecast bad weather with amazing accuracy.

By Tuesday morning the wind was shrieking and rattling the house worse than ever. My bedroom window was completely covered with ice and snow, allowing in only a smidgen of sickly gray light. The terrible weather excited me, and I jumped out of bed, got dressed, and raced down the stairs.

There was no daylight coming in from the kitchen windows at all. All of the lights were on. I checked the Regulator clock on the wall to make sure I hadn't gotten up too early.

Finishing up my customary breakfast of oatmeal, I asked my mother, "Kin I go out an' play in the blizzard?"

The rest of the family got a huge chuckle out of that. My father opened the kitchen door leading out into the storm porch. A surge of icy air rushed into the kitchen. Pushing hard, he tried to open the outer storm door. The door cracked open only three inches and no further, blocked by a huge snow drift. "Ain't nobody goin' out today," he said.

"Why do you have to keep looking out there?" my mother asked him. "Close that door. You're letting all the heat out."

My father came back in and threw another chunk of wood in the kitchen stove.

"How we gonna get out?" I asked.

"I'll shovel out when this thing blows over," the old man said.

My mother frowned. "How are you going to shovel snow if you can't get outside?"

He had to think about that one.

The storm raged on all that day. I ran from window to window, trying to get a glimpse of the blizzard, but all I could see was thick flying snow. There was plenty to hear, though. The windows never stopped rattling, and the wind howled in the chimney like a forlorn wolf.

Everyone began searching for something to do. My mother sat at the living-room library table, clipping recipes from back issues of *Woman's Day* magazines. My sister went upstairs and rearranged her bedroom furniture four or five times. The old man decided that it was high time he repaired the bedroom alarm clock that had quit working a year ago, and he soon had springs, gears, and screws scattered all over the linoleum on the kitchen table. I stretched out on the living-room rug, selecting color schemes for pictures in my Edgar Bergen and Charlie McCarthy coloring book.

By late afternoon my father had reassembled the alarm clock, confident that it was now in working order.

My mother came into the kitchen to make coffee, and she reached down and picked up a loose spring and two small gears from the floor. "Don't these go in that clock?" she asked, handing the spare parts to my father.

The old man hated to be criticized on his repair projects. "Aw, th'clock don't need those *!!@# things," he snapped, tossing the gear and the springs on the table.

My mother got indignant. "Oh? Well, wind it up and see if it runs."

He wound up the clock. It didn't run.

"Hah!" my mother gloated.

The phrase "cabin fever" hadn't been coined yet, but that's what was setting in.

After a supper of warmed-up hash I tried the radio again with no luck. We brought out Pick-Up Sticks and everyone got down on the rug to play. My mother came in last in every game because her hands were too shaky worrying about the blizzard.

"If the snow doesn't stop soon, we're going to run out of food," she said. "Although . . . I guess I could thin out the hash and make it stretch."

"Thin out the hash!" my sister exclaimed. "You're kidding! It's bad enough the way it is!"

My mother glared at her. "Listen, you're lucky to *get* hash. People in China are starving." The incontestable "People in China" rebuttal was always employed whenever anyone complained about the food in our house.

My father cast an uneasy eye at the wood box in the corner of the kitchen. "We kin go hungry fer awhile, but if this storm don't let up pretty soon, we're gonna run out of wood fer the stoves."

An hour later we noticed that it had become very quiet. "The windows aren't rattlin' anymore," Esther said. "Maybe the storm is over."

The old man went out into the storm porch and again pushed hard against the outside door. This time it wouldn't budge at all. He came back into the kitchen and went to the stove, lifted up a lid, and put his ear down to listen to the wind. "It ain't over. Th'wind's still blowin'. It's quiet because th'house is buried."

On Wednesday the morning light filtering in through the coat of ice on my bedroom window was stronger. I couldn't hear any wind, only a loud thumping noise coming from downstairs. I dressed and went downstairs.

The door leading into the storm porch was open, and my father was rearing back and battering his shoulder against the outside door. It was open a crack, with snow visible all the way from top to bottom. The doorway was completely beneath the snow.

"You're going to break your shoulder if you keep that up," my mother told him.

"You gotta better idea?"

"Go upstairs and crawl out through one of the bedroom windows and onto the porch roof. It can't be much of a drop to the ground if the snow is that deep."

The old man took a breather from battering the door. "All them windows got storm windows on 'em, fastened from the outside. I'd have to break one to get out. Glass fer them windows ain't cheap."

"It's better than starving to death," my mother replied.

My father went back to bashing the door. When his shoulder gave out he kicked the door, forcing it open another few inches. Finally, he took the snow shovel and dug into the wall of snow between the door and the frame, pulling snow inside onto the porch floor. After an hour he had carved out a pocket in the snow large enough to allow him to stand outside. He jabbed the blade of the shovel over his head and broke through to daylight. There was an eight-foot drift up against the house, but the sky was clear. The blizzard was over.

I jumped up and down with excitement. "Let's dig a tunnel out to the street!"

The old man said, "First we gotta get to th'woodshed."

The snow in our yard wasn't as high as the drift that covered the door, but it was still plenty deep. My father spent the morning digging a deep trench toward the woodshed. I was bundled up in my snowsuit and stood behind him as he shovelled, but I couldn't see a thing because the top of the trench was way over my head. The old man took a break and put me on his shoulders so I could look around.

The backyard didn't look like our backyard at all. It was a sea of snow.

"Where's the woodshed?" I asked.

"It's there somewhere," the old man said.

It was a monumental job to locate and excavate the woodshed door and get it open. But it had to be done because we needed wood for the stoves, and my father also had to retrieve his snowshoes and toboggan from the shed in order to make a trip downtown to get food.

The grocery list was longer than usual because my mother was convinced that another blizzard was on the way. After filling up the wood box my father put me on the toboggan, and we headed for downtown Ishpeming.

Our street was completely clogged with snow, and as I remember, it didn't get plowed for days. The downtown streets were a priority. The old man clumped along on his snowshoes, pulling me on the toboggan down the middle of the street. The snow was so deep that the houses appeared to have sunk into the ground; in most cases only the second stories were visible. Garages couldn't be seen at all. Telephone poles were short, their ice-encrusted wires drooping in the snowdrifts.

The blizzard had moved on, and now men were everywhere, digging out. Division Street, one of Ishpeming's two main thoroughfares, bustled with activity. The storefronts were covered with snowdrifts, but storekeepers had already hired school kids (naturally, school was cancelled) to dig out their stores. The wind-driven snow was hard-packed and tough to shovel, so hard in fact, that in many cases tunnels had been dug to the store entrances without concern for cave-ins.

Everyone was on skis or snowshoes. It was easy to tell which stores had the most customers by the number of skis and snowshoes jammed into the snow by the door.

Not a car was moving, only a lone bulldozer with a large plow blade, struggling with the near-impossible task of clearing Division Street. There was just too much snow. Drifts towered over the plow blade, and the snow had to be scraped away in layers.

I leaned forward on the toboggan and pointed at a man on snowshoes walking ahead of the bulldozer with a long iron rod, plunging it down into the snow every few feet. "What's he doing?"

"He's lookin' for buried cars so the plow don't hit 'em," my father said.

We went into Cox's Grocery Store where we had a charge account. A crowd of men with grocery lists from their wives were all jabbering at old man Cox, trying to get orders filled. Everyone had run out of food.

Cox stopped what he was doing and made an announcement. "I can only give everybody one can of evaporated milk. I ain't got much left. No fresh milk at all. Got no eggs either."

A chorus of groans.

"I guess yer gonna get toast fer breakfast tomorrow," my old man told me.

Nothing wrong with that, I thought. If blizzards stopped the milk supply and I couldn't eat oatmeal, then I was in favor of more blizzards.

After an hour's wait—Cox was the only one serving customers—we finally got our groceries. I then discovered the real reason the old man took me along. It was my job to hang onto the grocery bags so they wouldn't fall off the toboggan into the snow.

On the way back down Division Street my father stopped to talk to Toivo Jarvi who was standing up to his knees in snow because he had neither snowshoes or skis. "Howzit goin', Toivo?"

Toivo didn't look too happy. "It's goin' t'hell iz where it's goin'."

"Whatza matter?"

"I gotta peach of a hangover . . . an' I can't find my car."

My father grinned. "Ya don't remember where ya left it?"

Toivo shook his head. "I'm workin' day shift at the mine, an' Monday afternoon I stopped here at Bruno's place for a quick one after work. Well, it wuz more than a quick one, an' after awhile I came outta the bar to go home, but it wuz blowin' an' snowin' so hard I went back in Bruno's. Had to stay there all day yesterday an' last night, me an' five, six other guys an' Bruno. We only got dug out this mornin'."

"Well, ya could'a got stuck in worse places. Bruno's got a lotta booze."

"He *had* a lotta booze. Me an' them other guys tried to drink it all up. After awhile we got hungry, but there wuz nuthin' to eat in the bar 'cept potato chips and pickles. Would'a paid ten dollars fer a pasty."

My father pointed at the bulldozer plow slowly making its way down the street. "Well, looks like they'll dig yer car out pretty quick."

"Hell, I don' know if it's even *on* this street. Now that I think about it, I don't even remember where I started drinkin'. Fer all I know I might'a parked th'car over on First Street by them beer gardens over there. The old lady's gonna kill me. That's a new car."

As we moved off, Toivo was shouting to the man with the iron rod, "Take it easy with that *!!#@ thing. My new car is down there somewheres."

On Thursday morning the *Daily Mining Journal* paper boy finally navigated down our street on skis, and we were just now able to read the news about the blizzard. During the height of the storm a fire had broken out in downtown Marquette. Firemen, hampered by high winds, freezing temperatures, and deep snow, couldn't contain the blaze, and the fire had quickly spread from building to building, gutting much of the downtown area.

"Damage was estimated at . . ." The old man paused, moving his lips as he counted zeroes. "Four hundred grand! Kin you imagine that? The whole town must've burned down."

My mother pointed at the bowl of oatmeal sitting in front of me that had a big ugly puddle of canned milk in the middle of it. "Eat it, it's good for you."

I tried a spoonful and grimaced; canned milk was much worse than fresh milk. "If I finish it, kin I go out an' play? The sun's out and the snow's gonna melt."

"I don't think we have to worry about the snow melting anytime soon," my mother told me.

Someone rapped urgently on the door. My mother put down her dishrag and opened it.

Bertha Maki came bustling in. "You won't *believe* who was visiting Louella Bundsen when the blizzard hit. He couldn't leave, had to stay with her for three days in that dinky little one-bedroom place!" She stopped to catch her breath before continuing.

The old man rolled his eyes and lowered his head back into the newspaper. My mother pointed at me and then the stairs.

A County Fair and the Crash of Doom

My old man had that sly look whenever he had something up his sleeve. He licked the seam on the roll-your-own Bull Durham cigarette—the only kind he could afford during the Depression—stuck the cigarette in his mouth and torched it with a kitchen match. He took a long drag and blew a smoke ring. "Whaddaya say we take in the county fair on Saturday?"

"Whut's a county fair?" I asked. At age seven I didn't know much.

"People bring horses, cows, pigs, sheep, chickens, an' other stuff to show off an' win ribbons. There's lots to eat, too."

Lots to eat—for me those were magic words. At that age I needed plenty of calories to support my growth rate of an inch per week. We had just finished a supper of cold cheese sandwiches, sliced cucumbers, and buttermilk, and I was still hungry. My mother had cranked up a batch of homemade vanilla ice cream, and I was waiting at the table for some of that.

She began dishing up the ice cream. "We can't afford to go to any county fair."

But the old man was in an expansive mood and would not be denied. "All it'll take is a coupl'a bucks outta the sugar bowl."

"That's school clothes money," my mother replied sharply.

The old man leaned over to me with a conspiratorial grin and said, "Whaddaya think? Would'ja rather have cotton candy or new underwear?"

"Whut's cotton candy?" I asked.

"It's pure sugar," my mother snapped. "It'll rot your teeth."

Whenever she said, "It'll rot your teeth," I knew she was talking about something good. "I wanna go to the county fair an' get some cotton candy," I pleaded.

"There'll be lots of patchwork quilts," the old man cleverly added, glancing at my mother, who was big on that sort of thing. "An' women bring cookies and cakes and stuff like that, too. You can find out how good them other women are at baking."

"If we go to the county fair, will they gimme a piece of cake?" I asked.

My father chuckled. "You touch one a them cakes, them women'll slap yer hand good. Only the judges eat that cake."

My mother was noticeably weakening. "It's all the way to Marquette. How would we get there?" We didn't own a car.

"I kin get us a ride," the old man said, like he'd already planned the whole thing.

Saturday morning my mother fidgeted restlessly with the slip straps under her new summer dress. For the tenth time she leaned over and peered into the shopping bag, trying to decide if she should take a few more cheese sandwiches along to the fair.

Worried, she said to the old man, "He won't be drinking beer at this hour, will he?"

"Naw, Buffey don't drink as much as people think."

My Uncle Bill Buffey, the lone Gaelic branch in our family tree, was giving us a ride to the county fair. Buffey was a handsome Irishman who drove cars too fast, smoked tailor-made cigarettes, and had a gift of gab that charmed the socks off anyone within range of his voice. Our Finnish relatives couldn't understand why my father's sister Martha had taken an Irishman for a husband. After all, there were plenty of eligible Finn bachelors in Ishpeming. Finns were supposed to marry Finns.

A shrill wolf whistle pierced the still air.

My mother looked up, startled. "What on earth is that?"

"That's Buffey's car horn," my father said.

She peered nervously through the living-room lace curtains. "A horn can make a sound like that?"

Uncle Bill bounded up on the porch and banged on the kitchen door. "Anybody home in there? Let's get going! We ain't got all day!" He charged into the kitchen and without warning took my mother by the waist and whirled her around a few times before putting her back on the floor.

"Do that again, and I'll pound you good," my mother said evenly.

We proceeded out to Buffey's car, a gleaming, jet-black, two-door '37 Ford with white-sidewall tires and a foxtail hanging from a long, shiny radio aerial. My Aunt Martha and little cousin Karen stood alongside the open door as my folks and I piled into the back seat.

Buffey rammed the car into gear and blew the horn at no one in particular. The loud wolf whistle startled Bruno, a surly neighborhood German shepherd-collie mix, who growled and began chasing the Ford down the street, intent on biting the tires.

Buffey thrust a fist out the window and yelled at Bruno. "Bite one of those white-sidewalls, you mangy mutt, and I'll stop and pull out all your teeth!"

Karen stood up on the front seat and faced us in the back, solemnly staring at me. "I'm gonna ride on the Ferris wheel."

I said nothing. I didn't like talking to girls and Karen, in particular. She had Shirley Temple looks, but the similarity ended there. Her ice-blue eyes signalled that she was always one up on you.

"You don't know what a Ferris wheel is, do you?" she said.

"Sure I do."

"It goes round and round and up and down. It's scary. You'll pee your pants."

"I will not!" I cried indignantly. Where did a punky five-year-old girl learn to talk like that?

Out on the two-lane highway Buffey showed us what the Ford would do, cranking it up to fifty. We passed the time identifying the makes of cars in the oncoming traffic.

Buffey was an expert on cars. "Here comes a '38 Packard," he announced.

I was pretty good myself. At a distance of half a mile I neatly scored a '37 Pontiac.

When we got tired of that we recited all of the Burma Shave signs in unison, chanting:

> DON'T STICK YOUR ELBOW
> OUT TOO FAR
> IT MIGHT GO HOME
> IN ANOTHER CAR.
> BURMA SHAVE

> SHAVING BRUSHES
> WILL SOON BE TRIMMIN'
> THOSE SCREWY HATS
> WE SEE ON WIMMIN.
> BURMA SHAVE

Buffey made one up about a tractor salesman and the farmer's daughter, which I didn't get. Aunt Martha told him to shut up and just drive.

Large, brightly colored tents dotted the landscape at the fairgrounds. After impatiently blowing the wolf whistle to scatter the pedestrians, Buffey parked the car, and we followed the mob of people streaming toward the entrance. Before we even got inside, my mother was complaining about the price of admission shown on the sign at the wooden ticket booth. "Twenty-five cents just to get in? That's robbery!"

We coughed up the money anyway and went inside, inhaling the exotic fragrant blend of hot popcorn, sawdust, sizzling hot dogs, and fresh cow plop.

One stand with a big whirling tub was making strange fluffy pink stuff. I instinctively knew it was cotton candy. The old man fished out a nickel and bought me some.

"It tastes just like sugar," I said.

"I told you so. It'll rot your teeth," my mother said.

At any county fair a visit to the animal tents was mandatory. A mama pig lay on her side, acting indifferent to the crowd while feeding her hungry litter. There were huge groomed and clipped draft horses that gazed down at us with liquid brown eyes. White rabbits, black rabbits, spotted rabbits, and flop-eared rabbits nibbled on carrots and lettuce. Goats munched on the same fare, not tin cans as I had been led to believe. Red hens, orange hens, brown hens, and speckled hens glowered at us suspiciously, convinced that we were going to steal their eggs.

In the fruit and vegetable tent the old man exclaimed, "They're givin' blue ribbons fer rhubarb fer crissake. Looks just like the stuff growin' wild in our back yard."

"I need a cold one," Buffey declared after awhile. We drifted back to the midway. Uncle Bill got his beer and we moved along with the dusty crowd.

DIRECT FROM MINNESOTA!
Dan Dervish and his daredevil drivers
See the CRASH OF DOOM!
You won't believe your eyes!
The Grandstand 4 PM

These posters were everywhere, complete with a stunning color illustration of lantern-jawed Dan Dervish in a Flash-Gordon helmet, clutching a very large steering wheel with gloved hands. His grey eyes stared coolly from behind oversized goggles, conveying the message that he was in full control of whatever he was driving.

"I gotta see that!" Buffey declared. "Those guys barrel around that track at seventy miles an hour, I'll bet."

My mother scowled at the poster. "Why would anyone spend good money watching a bunch of maniacs running into each other? Let's go and see the sewing."

Inside a large crafts tent were display after display of quilts, lace curtains, embroidered doilies, tablecloths, wall hangings, and other handmade items of every description. One blue-ribbon prize winner was made by a woman who lived alone on the Yellow Dog River. She had apparently spent her long winters creating a mammoth wall hanging of a large-mouth bass leaping out of the water. The water was made from scraps of worn overalls, and the fish scales were hundreds of Stroh's beer-bottle caps, ample proof that winters on the Yellow Dog River were long and lonely.

I worked on a taffy sucker as we proceeded toward the center of the fairgrounds. My mother realized that her cheese sandwiches would melt in the heat and began them passing out. With this solid underpinning of nutritious food, I negotiated for a candy apple for dessert.

A man chewing on a soggy cigar pointed a bamboo cane at a series of small paper targets beyond his makeshift counter where several .22 rifles lay. "Awright, awright, step right up here an' hit the bulls-eye. Three shots fer a dime."

Karen tugged at Buffey's trouser leg. "Get me a teddy bear, Daddy."

The barker knew that he had a live one on the hook. "Yeah, Daddy, don'cha wanna win a teddy bear for the pretty li'l girl?"

Buffey took up the challenge and flipped a dime at the barker. He grabbed a scarred rifle, aimed at one of the pea-sized bulls-eyes, and blasted away. All three of his shots missed the bulls-eye.

Buffey took the Lord's name in vain and slapped another dime in the barker's open palm.

"That's twenty cents already," Martha reminded him.

Buffey's barrage missed again, and Karen rolled her eyes in utter dismay.

My father stepped up to the rifles. "How many bulls-eyes do ya haf'ta hit t'get a bear?"

The barker relit his cigar. "One bulls-eye for the baby bear, two for the mama bear, and three bulls-eyes for the big daddy bear."

The old man picked up every rifle, one after another, looked each one over carefully, and then selected one. He dug in his pocket for a dime. My mother didn't say a word; she had seen him shoot before.

He hit the bulls-eye on the first shot.

The barker was impressed. "Hey, hey, we gotta marksman here!" He handed my father the second cartridge and puffed furiously on his cigar, raising smoke to obscure the view of the targets.

The old man got another bulls-eye.

The barker's jaw dropped, but he recovered quickly, seizing the opportunity to draw a crowd. "Folks, we got Sergeant York here! Step up an' see him try to hit three bulls-eyes in a row!"

People stopped to watch. A fat man, beet red from the sun and the Fox Deluxe beer he was guzzling, drew up close, exercising his trigger finger in anticipation.

The last bullet struck a third bulls-eye. The barker, uneasy now, handed my father a large, brilliant-yellow plush teddy bear and promptly jerked the .22 from his hand before the old man decided to try his luck again.

Karen clutched the teddy bear, and we moved on toward the

grandstand. Feeling the pangs of hunger again, I talked the old man into buying me a hot dog.

It was close to four o'clock as we joined the crowd filing into the grandstand. The thundering of unmuffled, powerful engines told us that Dan Dervish and his crew were tuning up for their grim task of cheating death. We bought tickets and seated ourselves on the grandstand benches.

Out on the grassy infield was a line-up of bizarre automobiles. The fenders were severely mashed or missing entirely. Strips of white tape crisscrossed the windshields. There was no side or rear window glass, and all the doors were welded shut. Bumpers consisted of thick wooden planks. These were not Sunday-driving machines.

Their hoods were up, and men in dark blue coveralls leaned over the engines, making last-minute adjustments.

VAARRROOOOMMM!
VAARRROOOOMM!   VAARRROOOOMM!

The engines alternately roared to a high crescendo and then cut back to a rumbling idle, blowing out plumes of oily blue smoke that drifted over the grandstand. I sniffed it. This was not ordinary car exhaust; these babies were burning something besides gasoline.

Finally, the blue-clad men crawled in through the driver's-side windows, and the cars roared in a procession onto the track directly in front of the grandstand. A voice boomed from the loudspeakers.

"LADEEZ AND GENTLEMEN, ALLOW ME TO PRESENT
DAN DERVISH AND HIS WHEELS OF DEATH!"

The ground trembled as the drivers, with exquisite timing, mashed the accelerators and the line of cars thundered away, rocketing counterclockwise around the track. Within seconds they roared past the grandstand in tight formation, a scant six inches separating front and back bumpers. They sped around the track, doing a few more laps, then suddenly spun 180 degrees in perfect precision and performed the same exercise in reverse gear. The crowd gawked. Beer drinkers stood frozen, the cups halfway to their mouths.

But Dervish's Daredevils were only warming up. The cars began executing intricate weaving maneuvers, some in high gear, others in reverse. Then, all but a pair of roadsters pulled into the infield and stopped. The two remaining cars, V-8 engines idling fitfully, sat on the track while a well-developed blonde in red-spangled tights stepped up, smiled at the grandstand, and opened the rumble seats of both cars. Flashing fishnet-clad thighs, she climbed into one of the open rumble seats. The two cars tore off around the track side by side. As they came around on the first lap, travelling at sixty miles an hour, the blonde was standing on the rumble-seat, hair streaming and arms akimbo, the spangles on her red tights snapping in the wind.

"She's gonna switch cars," Buffey predicted in a hushed voice.

And that's exactly what happened. Just as the cars hurtled past the grandstand a second time—still neck and neck—the blonde lithely stepped from her seat in one car onto the rumble seat of the other. Everyone cheered, whistled, and clapped.

The action then paused, and the beer and peanut vendors noisily resumed their rounds through the stands. Everyone sensed that the stage had just been set for the final act. I got a sack of peanuts and waited for the Crash of Doom.

"LADEEZ AND GENTLEMEN. DAN DERVISH HIMSELF
WILL NOW ATTEMPT, FOR YOUR VIEWING PLEASURE, A
VERY DANGEROUS ACT.
THE GRAND FINALE, THE CRASH OF DOOM!
LET'S GIVE DAN A BIG HAND!"

Dan Dervish, tall and slim, dark hair slicked back, was dressed all in white. He bounced onto the track, took a bow in front of the grandstand, then donned a heavy helmet just like on the poster and crawled in through the window of one of the cars in the infield. Dervish fired up the engine and buzzed out onto the track. Like the rest, the car was stripped, dented, taped, and welded, but Buffey identified it immediately.

"It's a '37 Ford." he shouted. "He's gonna do it in a '37 Ford!" Buffey took a big slug of beer, eager to watch Dan Dervish perform the Crash of Doom in the same car that he drove.

In a cloud of dust and burning rubber, Dervish took off and roared around the track at high speed. He shot past the grandstand and stuck his arm out the window, waving jauntily to the crowd.

No sooner had he passed by us when members of his crew rushed beneath the grandstands and quickly began pushing out a large old car that had been hidden there. They positioned it crosswise on the track.

"Omigawd," Martha cried. "He's going to hit that car when he comes around!"

"It's a DeSoto," Buffey told us. "That's why they had to push it. DeSotos never run."

Dervish roared into the final turn and headed directly at the DeSoto sitting squarely on the track. But at the very last moment, without decelerating, he swerved violently to the infield side and with shrieking tires whipped around the parked car and proceeded around the track again. Coming around, he again headed straight for the DeSoto at high speed.

This time he hit the car broadside.

The force of the impact propelled the old DeSoto ten feet down the track, rolling it over onto its side. Ragged chunks of metal flew everywhere. A headlight tore loose and arced over into the infield.

The front end of Dervish's car was totally smashed. The hood had ripped off and landed close to the grandstands. Hot oil and water puddled in the dirt. A huge cloud of steam rose from the mangled radiator.

Women screamed. Men were tight-lipped and grim. A dangerous stunt maneuver had somehow gone terribly wrong.

Or had it? Lively march music blared over the loudspeakers. Dan Dervish pulled himself out of the destroyed car, yanked off his helmet, faced the grandstand, and victoriously threw his hands up in the air.

"LADEEZ AND GENTLEMEN, DAN DERVISH HAS JUST PERFORMED THE CRASH OF DOOM! GIVE HIM A BIG HAND!"

"It's a miracle," my mother said.

"It's a safety harness, is what it is," Buffey explained.

I said nothing, but I'd memorized every detail of the crash. Months later I would still be reenacting the feat in my backyard sandpile, using cast-iron toy cars.

We left the grandstand and moved toward the carnival rides. Suppertime had arrived, and my mother dealt out the last of the cheese sandwiches which we washed down with creme soda.

Buffey pointed. "You kids wanna ride bumper cars?"

"Yeah!" Karen shouted.

A couple dozen little electric rubber-bumpered cars were scooting around in an enclosed area. Drivers of all ages howled with insane glee as they whipped the steering wheels back and forth, recklessly and intentionally ramming everyone in their path. Sparks flew from the wheels as the cars crashed into one another.

Buffey bought three tickets, and he and Karen and I stepped up and selected three empty cars.

"Whut am I supposed to do?" I asked.

"Hit the other cars," Buffey said.

The only vehicles I'd ever piloted were my tricycle and scooter, but it didn't matter; skill was not a prerequisite with bumper cars. The concessionaire told me, "The gas petal's on the floor, kid, an' there's the steering wheel. Tha's all ya need to know."

I climbed in and tentatively put my foot on the accelerator. The car lurched out into the traffic and was immediately struck by several maniacs. I grasped the steering wheel and attempted to dodge cars, a practice I was to employ to good advantage in later years when I ventured onto the Los Angeles freeway system.

A little gray-haired lady rammed me broadside. "Get outta my way, kid!" she cackled.

"Watch out!" Buffey yelled as he hit me from the other side.

Karen used the direct approach. She hit me head on. "Got'cha, you big dummy!"

My car slowed momentarily from the head-on collision, and I pushed my legs out of the car, preparing to make a run for safety. The concessionaire immediately yelled at me. "Stay in the car, kid!"

I huddled down behind the wheel and hung on patiently while my car got swatted around like a hockey puck. Finally, the power was cut and the cars stopped. The ride was over.

"You're a pretty rotten driver," Karen commented as we got out of the cars.

The mass of miscellaneous food I'd eaten had become seriously scrambled in my stomach, and I was ready to search for a deserted patch of weeds, but before I had the opportunity, Karen pulled me onto a seat on the Caterpillar. This was an insidious machine that whips its hapless occupants around a circular rolling track. Sometime after the ride begins and you think you've just about had enough, a large shroud envelopes the cars and riders, plunging everyone into darkness while it continues its winding ride. For what seemed like days, we undulated, banked, and rolled in total blackness. All the while Karen had a death grip around my neck and was screaming in my ear. When the car slowed and the cover was pulled back to reveal blessed daylight, she cried, "Let's do it again!"

But instead we went over to the Ferris wheel. I looked up at the rickety network of long, spidery beams soaring high into the sky. At the very top, swinging back and forth precariously, was a tiny seat just like the one we were getting into.

"Are we goin' up there?" I asked the grubby operator dressed in an oily undershirt and overalls who was clamping a wooden bar across our laps. He didn't answer but instead spat a wad of tobacco into the dirt and pushed a long iron lever, throwing the Ferris wheel in gear. An ancient engine connected by belts to the large wheel belched blue smoke, and we lurched backward and upward. The wheel turned in fits and starts while the other riders were being loaded on. Then the beams and bolts creaked in unison, and the wheel began to spin.

We went up, up, up to the very top and then plunged down. Lake Superior, the State of Michigan, and a large part of Canada revolved before my eyes. I breathed a ragged sigh of relief when we spun down to ground level, but then we shot up again. This continued for many revolutions. The Ferris wheel operator, spotting my panic, gave me a wide snaggle-toothed grin every time I went by.

We climbed high once more, and when we were right at the very top, the wheel braked to a stop. Our seat swung wildly back and forth. I white-knuckled the wooden bar.

Karen pointed and yelled. "Look! I can see my dad down there!"

Looking down was a big mistake. The seat was squeaking and pitching fitfully. The whole Ferris wheel was swaying and wobbling from the wind coming off Lake Superior.

Then it all came up. A pungent gusher of cheese, candy apple, cream soda, hot dog, cotton candy, and other unidentifiable substances soared majestically into the air and downward.

"You want to see everything he ate?" Karen asked my mother. "It's over there, all over the ground."

"No, that's okay."

"He even got a couple of people right on top of the head."

"Yes, I know, Karen."

Buffey looked me over critically. "Lemme give him a sip of my beer. That always settles *my* stomach."

"I don't think so," my mother said. "I guess it's about time we headed for home."

Footsore and sunburned, we plodded wearily across the grassy field that served as a parking lot. We got into the Ford, and Buffey inched his way along in the long line of dusty cars leaving the fairgrounds.

"That guy Dervish knows what he's doing, all right," Buffey said. "Using a '37 Ford. This car can really take it." He patted the steering wheel affectionately. "You notice his engine was still running after the crash?"

"I think it was all some kind of trick," Martha said.

"I don't see how that woman got all of those beer-bottle caps to make that fish," my mother said. "Women don't drink like that."

My old man, intent on paying our share of the trip expenses, reached over the front seat and handed Buffey a dime for a gallon of gas.

Buffey pulled into a gas station and gave instructions to the attendant to pump in ten cents worth of gas, clean the windshield, and to check the oil and water and the air pressure in the tires.

My stomach, now completely empty, was recuperating quite nicely, once again ready for action. I pointed at a sign in the gas-station window.

"Ma . . . they're selling Popsicles here."

First Romance

*O*ur fourth-grade teacher, Miss Flintlock, didn't begin that particular December morning with her customary blitzkrieg of orders and ultimatums. In fact, she was in such a good mood that her thick makeup cracked under the strain of a rare smile as she grasped the hand of the girl standing at her desk.

"Class, I want to introduce a new student, Carol Browning. Her family just moved here from Grand Rapids. I know you will all make her feel welcome."

She moved here from Grand Rapids? That was incredible. Nobody in Michigan ever moved north, and certainly not up here to the buckle of the snow belt. In fact, during World War II, any right-thinking person able to scrape up the train fare was heading *out of*, not into, Upper Michigan, going south to Detroit, Milwaukee, or Chicago where big bucks were being made building tanks, guns, and fighter planes.

Roy (a.k.a. Piggy) O'Neal, sitting directly in front of me, decided to give the new girl his own personal welcome. He ducked his head down, put a grubby hand over his mouth, and issued his famous, low-pitched, slobbery pig grunt, which we'd all heard and enjoyed on the playground but never in the classroom. The boys snickered appreciatively at Piggy's derring-do.

Unfortunately for Piggy, Miss Flintlock also heard the grunt, and her good mood evaporated. "Roy O'Neal, stand up!"

Piggy slowly got to his feet.

Flintlock pointed a gnarled finger at an empty desk in the front row, which was within easy range of her wooden yardstick. "Up here. And bring your books and pencil box with you."

Piggy, realizing that he was about to do hard time in what we called the "Hot Seat," grumbled under his breath as he slowly emptied his desk and reluctantly shuffled up to the empty desk at the front of the room.

Flintlock leaned over Piggy, her sharp, powdered nose a scant inch from his face. "Roy, you're going to sit there for the remainder of the year where I can keep an eye on you." She turned to the new girl. "Carol, go back and take the desk that Mr. O'Neal has just vacated."

On long graceful legs the new girl slowly sashayed down the aisle toward me. She had large, thick-lashed brown eyes. Dark braids coiled like a halo around her head. Her pert nose was lightly sprinkled with freckles, like flecks of sunshine. I couldn't believe my luck. This vision of loveliness was actually going to sit right in front of me for the rest of the year.

She looked me right in the eye and said in a soft sultry voice, "Hello."

Having had no experience carrying on a dialogue with a beautiful woman, I lost my ability to speak. All that came out of my mouth was, "Ghaaagh."

I didn't remember much of the next hour, only that the back of Carol Browning's neck was the most beautiful back of any neck I'd ever seen, certainly much *cleaner* than Piggy O'Neal's. We sailed through geography class. Miss Flintlock could have told us that the Amazon River emptied into Lake Superior, and I would have accepted it as fact. Nothing mattered. I was in love.

Up to that point in my life I'd ranked girls right up there with boiled carrots at the top of my hate list. Why I'd suddenly gone soft in the head over this one was too scary to analyze.

At the ten-thirty recess the boys elbowed the girls aside and raced for the cloakroom, yelling and punching each other as they pulled on their coats. It had been only yesterday that I'd been flaunting my loutishness right there along with the rest of them. But love changes you. This time I rose quietly from my seat and followed Carol Browning out of the room.

SKRITCH, SKRITCH, SKRITCH, SKRITCH

She turned around. "Is that you?"

"Whut?"

"Is that you making that noise?"

"Whut noise?" The legs of my corduroy knickers had rubbed together for so long that I didn't notice the sound any more.

"Are you making fun of me, too? Like that dumb kid who made the pig noise?"

Ida Lillywhite, the class intellectual, turned to Carol and said in her dry, witty tone, "He doesn't do it on purpose. It's his knickers. It sounds like he's sawing wood with his legs."

The fourth-grade girls all thought that Ida's remark was extremely clever. They went into the cloakroom cackling like a bunch of hens, taking Carol Browning with them.

"Ma, I want a pair of long pants."

My mother was sitting next to the wood stove in the living room, darning socks. "You've got a pair of long pants."

"Yeah, but they're church pants." Sunday-school clothes were off limits for rest of the week. "I want a pair of long pants to wear to school."

"You've got two pair of knickers."

"I hate knickers. They make a funny sound."

My mother peered over her glasses. "What funny sound?" She didn't notice it either.

"When I walk, the legs rub together, makin' this zit, zit, zit sound. None of the other boys wear knickers anymore. I been wearin' 'em a hunnert years."

"Those knickers are still in good shape. They'll last you for at least two more years yet."

That was the trouble with corduroy knickers; they were indestructible. Mine were living proof. We lived right next to the railroad tracks where the ore trains rumbled by. After countless hours of grubbing around on the tracks amid splintery railroad ties and flinty chunks of iron ore, my knickers were still in prime condition. One time, in a pitched iron-ore battle with the French-Italian gang, I took a direct hit in the seat of the pants from a fist-size chunk of ore. I couldn't sit down for a week, but there wasn't so much as a scuff on the knickers.

I couldn't even outgrow them. As I got taller, the elastic leg bottoms merely rode up higher on my calf, which was perfectly acceptable for knickers.

"There'll be plenty of time for long pants when you get into high school," my mother said, putting an end to the conversation.

The Central Grade School in Ishpeming took a strong position on English-language proficiency. Each month we suffered through a spelling bee and not any old bush-league spelling bee, either. You had to master multisyllable jawbreakers like exaggerate, overzealous, and mythological—words that you wouldn't normally throw into casual conversation while shooting marbles in the dirt. The spelling bees began with the kids standing around the perimeter of the classroom, like criminals against a firing squad wall, except that Flintlock fired words instead of bullets. Anyone that missed a word was out of the running and had to sit down. This continued, with increasingly harder words, until only one kid was left standing. As an incentive, Miss Flintlock awarded a twenty-five-cent defense stamp to the winner.

I never was much good at sports. I couldn't hit a baseball, my marbles game was truly laughable, and in a mumbletypeg match all the other kids watched me to see if I was going to stab myself with the knife.

But I wasn't bad at spelling. During the spelling bee that December I breezed along with little difficulty. As the afternoon wore on, one kid after another bit the dust until finally there were just two of us left. I was pitted against Ida Lillywhite, the same wise-guy girl who only the week before, in front of all of the fourth-grade girls, had made a complete fool of me with her cruel knickers remark.

We began the final round. Miss Flintlock said, "Ida, spell 'fragmentation.'"

Ida didn't bat an eye. "F-r-a-g-m-e-n-t-a-t-i-o-n."

Flintlock nodded her approval and turned to me. "Gerald, spell 'glamorous.'"

I almost blew the match right then and there. The word triggered an involuntary reaction, and I glanced over at Carol Browning sitting at her desk. She'd been eliminated in an early round, but with looks like that who had to know how to spell?

The corners of Carol's mouth turned up. She was smiling at me.

I froze up like a cigar-store Indian. Ida Lillywhite, concluding that I was stuck on "glamorous," smelled victory and began to smirk.

"Gerald, did you hear the word?" Miss Flintlock asked.

"Yes, ma'am." With a mighty effort I pulled myself together. "G-l-a-m-o-r-o-u-s."

Flintlock nodded, and Ida's smirk faded.

Ida and I traded word for word until Flintlock said, "Ida, spell 'ridiculing.'"

"R-i-d-i-c-u-l-e-i-n-g."

Miss Flintlock shook her head. "That's wrong. The proper spelling is r-i-d-i-c-u-l-i-n-g."

At the time, if I had known the concept of irony, I would have thought it ironic that Ida Lillywhite was so good at ridiculing but couldn't spell it.

Miss Flintlock handed me the twenty-five-cent defense stamp. "You're the winner."

The class clapped politely, as they'd been taught to do. The scattered applause helped deaden the noise my knickers made as I went back to my desk.

Carol turned around in her seat. "Wow! I didn't know you were such a good speller." She gave me her high-voltage smile again, showcasing the irresistible dimple in her right cheek.

That did it. I was truly smitten. The gum on the defense stamp melted in my hand.

The next day we were no sooner seated when Miss Flintlock looked at me and pointed to the cloakroom door. "Gerald, you know you're not supposed to wear overshoes in the classroom. Go remove them right now."

Now permanently assigned to the Hot Seat, Piggy O'Neal had nothing to lose, so he turned around and gave me a bold piggy grunt.

I clumped to the cloakroom, grumbling to myself. If I'd been wearing long pants, she would have never noticed the boots I had on over my shoes. But with knickers, they stuck out like hip waders. Carol Browning was an inch taller than me, and the boots neatly cut down her height advantage, but Flintlock, with her senseless, bureaucratic dress-code, had inadvertently squelched my plan. I took off the boots and returned to my desk, shorter but wiser.

The day dragged on. Finally, in late afternoon, after putting the whole class into a deep stupor by reading a detailed account of the major battles of the French and Indian War, Miss Flintlock stopped and took off her glasses. That was the signal. We rose as one, ready to bolt for home.

"Just a minute," Flintlock said. "I need two volunteers to clap erasers."

"Volunteers" was a complete misnomer. Flintlock customarily waited two milliseconds before drafting someone. I was ten feet from the safety of the cloakroom door, but the escape route was blocked by other bodies. I crouched behind Martha Hovi, a plump Finn girl, and carefully edged along the wall toward freedom.

"Gerald, how about you?"

I stopped dead in my tracks. Once your name was called, flight was useless.

"And Carol, why don't you help him."

Carol Browning was going to help me clap erasers? I quickly straightened up and walked tall to the front of the room to collect the box of dirty erasers.

Carol looked at me puzzled while we were putting on our coats in the cloakroom. "What's clapping erasers?"

"You never clapped erasers in Grand Rapids?"

"No."

"You take two erasers an' clap 'em together to get the chalk out. Lots'a kids don't know how to do it right, but I'll show ya my technique." Using the word 'technique' was brilliant, I thought.

I neglected to tell her that eraser clapping, a disagreeable task at best, was particularly hairy during the winter. We went down the hall, and I pushed open the outside door with great difficulty. The prevailing north wind screaming off Lake Superior had nothing to impede it as it whistled down Third Street toward the school. We stepped outside and were immediately pinned against the brick wall by a Force 10 bone-chiller.

"How long is this going to take?" Carol asked, her lips distorted by the frigid blast.

"Not long at all," I said, gallantly positioning myself to shield her from the wind. "Keep your hands in your pockets, and I'll do the whole thing." I casually unbuttoned my sheepskin jacket to show that the cold didn't phase me one bit.

Grabbing two erasers, I began to pound them together, sending up a huge cloud of chalk dust. "If ya clap 'em really hard, the chalk comes out in a hurry an' ya get done real quick." I shouted so that she could hear me above the wind.

It wasn't long before Carol looked down and noticed that she beginning to take on the appearance of a powdered-sugar donut. "Aughh! My new coat! You're getting chalk all over my new coat!" She began furiously brushing away the chalk dust. Eager to help, I dropped the erasers and started swatting the chalk dust off of her woolen bonnet. The only problem was that her head was still in it.

Carol jumped away. "Ow, ow . . . keep your hands off me!"

The eraser-clapping incident may have been a setback, but I wasn't easily discouraged. I concluded that a display of my intellectual skills would do the trick. Much to Miss Flintlock's surprise, I began volunteering to go up to the blackboard and chalk out solutions to the most difficult multiplication problems. I took to leaning forward at my desk and whispering my elevens and twelves, just loud enough so Carol Browning could hear. But nothing seemed to arouse her passions.

Then, the gods of probability took charge. On the Monday before Christmas vacation we drew names for Christmas presents.

"Write your name on the piece of paper that I've handed out," Flintlock announced. "Fold it, and pass it forward."

She put the names in a Santa-decorated box, swirled them around, and proceeded up and down the aisles, allowing each kid to draw one name.

I took a slip of paper from the box and opened it up.

In very elegant Palmer-Method penmanship was written

Carol Browning

My mother was in the kitchen, feeding Eight O'Clock beans into the coffee grinder.

"Ma, I need sum money."

"What for?"

"We drew names at school, an' I gotta buy a present fer a girl."

"Well, get me my purse. I think there's ten or fifteen cents in there."

"Kin I have fifty cents?"

She stopped cranking the grinder. "Fifty cents? What in the world are you talking about? You don't need fifty cents for that kind of present."

"Don'cha want me to buy a good present?"

She raised her eyebrows. "Have you got a crush on this girl?"

I felt my face turning red. "Aw, Ma. It's just sum dumb ol' girl."

"If it's just some dumb old girl, you don't need fifty cents. I'll give you twenty cents. Do you know what you're going to get her?"

"With twenty cents? Maybe a Japanese Zero model kit that she can put together herself." A present like that had possibilities, I thought. "If she doesn't know how to do it, I'll go over to her house an' show her."

"I don't think girls like to build model airplanes."

"Well, I seen a big little book called *Flash Gordon and the Mongo Planet of Doom*. There's movies on the page corners when you flip through the book. She ought'a go fer that."

"Why don't you get her one of those books of paper dolls?"

"I ain't gonna walk into no store an' buy paper dolls."

"Well, I'm not going to do it for you. If you want a present that a girl will like, you're going to have to walk into the store and buy it yourself."

The problem with living in a small town is that everyone knows you and knows your business. Of course, you know *them* and know *their* business, too, so maybe it all evens out. People from Ishpeming often travelled as far as Green Bay to purchase prophylactics and other such personal items. But being only nine years old I was at the mercy of the Ishpeming retailers.

Clyde, the teenage clerk in Linna's Drug Store, squinted down at me. "Ya wanna buy whut?"

"Uh . . . the paper-doll book in the window. It's for my sister for Christmas."

"Is that the same sister who went off to college last year?"

"Uh . . . well, it's really for my cousin."

"Uh-huh, well, that book of paper dolls cost a quarter. Ya got a quarter?" In all the years that Clyde sold me candy before the

Saturday-afternoon matinee, he rarely saw me with more than a nickel.

"All I got is twenny cents."

"Too bad."

"Whut would you buy a girl if you had twenny cents?" I asked Clyde.

"A bottle of beer an' a ride in my Ford."

I wandered over to the candy-display case. The war had inflated the price of candy, but twenty cents would still buy a lot—fifteen licorice sticks or sixty malted-milk balls, for instance. Enough to decay every tooth in Carol Browning's mouth. I didn't know what she liked, though, so I moved on.

Linnas had a Christmas display of lady's hair-care items: hair brushes with long sweeping handles of inlaid mother-of-pearl, genuine ebony-backed brushes, old-fashioned side combs with imitation tortoise shell handles. All out of my price range.

But nestled far back on the bottom shelf, all by itself, lay a small barrette of dark carved wood the exact shade of Carol Browning's eyes.

"How much is that?" I asked Clyde, pointing to the barrette.

"Twenty cents."

"I'll take it."

During the winter, recess out of doors on the playground was optional in bad weather. Of course, the fourth-grade boys, tough-as-nails U.P. men to the core, scoffed at sleet and sub-zero temperatures. Wednesday was the last school day before Christmas vacation, and the weather was particularly foul. We bravely stepped outside and huddled up against the school building, clustering together to share body heat and turning our backs to the wind to keep our fingers and noses from freezing and falling off.

Charlie Koski, our self-appointed leader, pulled his head deeper into his mackinaw. "I got Gloria Tavernini's name," he said. "Know whut I got her? One a them rubber snakes they sell over at Newberry's. She's gonna scream bloody murder when she opens that box."

The rest of us chuckled with mock enthusiasm and jumped up and down to get the feeling back in our feet.

Tommy Nardi chimed in. "I got ol' Becky Mobley's name. Got 'er some a them wax Mortimer Snerd teeth. That ought'a improve her looks." We all nodded and stomped our feet again.

Charlie Koski jabbed a mittened fist into my ribs. "Who's name didja draw?"

"Oh . . . jus' one a them dumb girls."

"Which one?"

"Carol Browning."

"Browning? The new one who sits right in front of you? Boy, if I wuz sittin' where you are, I'd pull one of her braids loose an' dip it right in the inkwell."

Everyone grunted in agreement and clapped their mittens together in a futile effort to draw the blood back in their fingers.

"Yeah, I might do that," I lied.

"Whadja get her?" Charlie asked.

"Oh . . . nuthin' much. Just somethin' for her hair."

"Did'ja get 'er one of them Harpo Marx wigs from Newberry's?" someone asked.

"Naw, just a barrette."

The gang stared at me in astonishment. It had never occurred to them to buy a girl a Christmas present that she might actually like.

The bell rang, and we trooped inside, secretly thankful to get out of the cold.

Miss Flintlock tapped her yardstick on the desk. "All right, girls and boys, we'll pass out presents now. After that you'll be dismissed until January."

Everyone cheered, and a festive holiday mood began to permeate the room. Two girls, assigned to be Santa's helpers, started passing out the presents.

I sat with my fingers locked on the edges of the desk, waiting for Carol's present to be delivered. Last night my mother put the barrette in a small box and neatly did it up in green tissue paper and a red ribbon.

Gloria Tavernini opened her gift from Charlie Koski and let out a piercing scream, flipping the box and the rubber snake onto the floor. Piggy O'Neal scooped the snake off the floor and stuffed it in his mouth. Everyone hooted. Even the teacher had to suppress a grin.

Becky Mobley took one look at the Mortimer Snerd teeth and quickly put the wrapping paper back on. She yelled something nasty at Tommy Nardi.

Other presents were opened. More laughter, screams, groans, and sharp words. Torn fragments of Christmas wrapping paper floated to the floor. Still, the little present in green tissue and red ribbon hadn't been delivered to the desk in front of me.

A small package was dropped on my desk, crudely wrapped in pink butcher paper and tied with white store string.

Inside was a small cake of wax, the kind used on the bottoms of skis. A note scribbled in pencil on tablet paper said:

STOP THE SNICKERS
WAX THOSE KNICKERS

The note wasn't signed. I looked up to see that all of the kids were watching me. They began laughing, and the laughter quickly built up to chortles and cackles. Everyone had been in on it.

Carol Browning turned around and smiled sadly at me. "It's okay. You can't help it."

I rose from my desk and walked rapidly to the cloakroom, my knickers SKRITCH, SKRITCH, SKRITCHing all the way. I went straight home, not caring if the little present in green tissue and red ribbon got delivered or not.

That was the beginning of my dark days. I had tried my best to fan a feeble spark of romance between Carol Browning and myself only to have it snuffed out by a pair of ugly pants that I was doomed to wear for the rest of my life. Even Christmas didn't matter. My mother, as usual, laid out a staggering selection of Yuletide goodies—homemade fruitcake, saffron bread, mincemeat pie, Philadelphia cream cheese, mixed nuts, and the hard candies only seen at Christmas. She even spiked my Christmas-morning Ovaltine with coffee.

But no amount of holiday feasting could pull me from the depths of this melancholic lethargy. Christmas presents that I'd lusted after all year—a giant-size can of Tinkertoys and the amazing Gilberts' chemistry set—didn't improve my mood. Although, while opening the chemistry set, my spirits were temporarily raised by the thought that if I ever found out the identity of the fourth-grade genius who had sent me the ski wax, I could learn how to build a stink bomb to place in his lunch box.

That morning, after all the presents were opened, my mother busied herself salvaging the reusable fragments of wrapping paper that littered the living-room carpet.

"Oh, look at this," she said to me. "Here's a present we missed; it's got your name on it. Must have gotten buried beneath the wrapping paper." She made it sound as though it was some kind of oversight, but no one in our family ever misplaced Christmas presents.

It was a soft package, probably some more stupid clothes. I

wouldn't have put it past one of my aunts to send me a pair of long underwear. Aunts did thing like that. I opened it up.

It was a pair of long pants.

"They're for school," my mother said. "I know how much you like those knickers, but I think it's time we replaced them."

Our whole fourth-grade class was experiencing a monumental post-holiday hangover. Piggy O'Neal's bloodshot eyes revealed that he had lost the habit of rolling out of bed at seven o'clock in the morning. Martha Hovi was cross because she'd gotten fatter than ever and had already grown out of her new purple Christmas dress with the puffed sleeves. For no good reason, Charlie Koski launched a spitball that smacked Ida Lillywhite squarely in the ear. Ida marched over and bashed Charlie right on top of the head with volume one of her new encyclopedia set. Miss Flintlock didn't react to any of this. Her eyes were bloodshot, too.

I glided noiselessly down the aisle toward my desk. Carol Browning looked up at me and smiled. "You got new pants."

Feeling very grownup, I merely nodded and sat down.

Miss Flintlock rapped on her desk. "All right, class, settle down. I hope you all had a nice Christmas, but it's time to get back to work. This morning we're going to tackle long division." Her chalk snapped crisply on the blackboard as she began laying out the first problem.

Whistling some nameless tune under my breath, I fished out my arithmetic book, tablet, and pencil from the desk. I sat up straight, ready to take on the worst that the dreaded long division had to offer.

There, right in front of my face, imbedded neatly in the back of Carol's braided hair, was a brown barrette the same color as her eyes.

Reflections of sunlight from the coat of ice on the windows lit up our classroom with a bright, diffused morning glow that we hadn't seen in a long time. The days were getting longer. Spring was just around the corner.

Spring. That's it, I thought. When the ground dried up I'd show her how to shoot marbles. What a great idea. How could she resist me after that?

Recollections of Milwaukee

In February, 1944, my parents decided to move from the U.P. to Milwaukee. I was ten years old and had always lived in the house where I was born, a quarter mile from the woods. Up to then the biggest city I'd ever been in was Marquette. I'd never seen a tall building or ridden on a streetcar or an escalator. For me this move was a *big, big* deal.

It was bitterly cold as my mother and I stood with several other people on the Ishpeming depot platform, waiting for the train. We could have waited inside where it was warm, but that wouldn't have qualified as real train watching, which was a serious pastime in the U.P. A truly dedicated train watcher stood on the edge of the platform, eyes peeled, competing with the other train watchers to be the first to catch sight of the locomotive.

I pointed down the tracks and yelled, "I see 'er!" At age ten my eyes were pretty sharp.

The new Chicago Northwestern Railroad's diesel streamliner, the 400, let loose with a horn blast as it approached the Third Street crossing. Moments later it pulled into the depot, the sleek coaches gliding to a stop.

A black man in a conductor's uniform hopped down from one of the coaches and placed a small wooden step on the platform so the passengers could disembark. If the truth be known, I had a secret fascination for the train depot and that was to see the black people. There weren't any in Ishpeming; the only ones I ever saw worked on the streamliner.

But the real reason my mother and I were at the station that day was to meet my father coming in on the train. During World War II thousands of Upper Michiganders were prowling the big cities, hoping to snap up lucrative wartime jobs. My old man was no exception. He had been down in Milwaukee scouting around for work.

Clutching his battered suitcase, he stepped off the train and leaned down to kiss my mother. "I found a job," he told her.

"What kind of job?"

"Assembly-line maintenance at International Harvester. They're buildin' tanks or sumthin' and hirin' anybody who comes through the door."

My mother grinned. "That must be why you got the job." This was in reference to the fact that the old man's only recent job experience was potato farming.

"When do you start?" she asked.

"The first of the month."

Her mouth fell open. "What? That's only three weeks from now. We can't sell the house and be ready to move by then."

"We'll haf'ta be." The old man handed me his suitcase so I could have the dubious honor of lugging it the five blocks to our house.

My pal Kippy and I were squatting next to the outside faucet on our house, dribbling water on an arsenal of snowballs—transforming them into lethal "ice balls"—in preparation for our upcoming planned ambush. Piggy O'Neal and his henchmen had built an impregnable snow fort down on First Street. Or so they thought. They would find out differently when they got a taste of our ice balls.

"We're gonna move," I said.

"Move? Whaddaya mean?"

"We're gonna go an' live in Milwaukee."

Kippy blinked at the news. "Why ya gonna do that?"

"Pop's gotta job. Lot'sa jobs there because of the war."

"Whut kind'a job?"

"Don't know exactly."

"Ya gonna come back after the war?" Kippy asked.

I hefted one of the ice balls for weight and balance. "I dunno. Pop sez there's always more work in the cities."

"Whut's yer pa gonna do with your house?"

"Sell it, I guess."

"How 'bout the stuff in yer house? Gonna take it all to Milwaukee?"

"No. Ma sez that we're gonna haf'ta leave most of it here. Sell it or give it away."

It was slowly dawning on me that I wouldn't be seeing Kippy much longer. He and I were lifelong pals. Together we'd learned the fine art of ski jumping, risking our necks using nothing more than toe-strap skis. Every Saturday afternoon we perched on the edge of our seats in the darkened balcony of the Ishpeming Theater, cheering on Gene Autry, Charles Starrett, and other cowboy heroes as they shot it out with the black-hatted rustlers and robbers. Shoulder to shoulder, we'd stood our ground on the ore-train tracks, pegging chunks of iron ore at the feared French-Italian gang anytime they encroached on our territory in South Ishpeming. Leaving my pal was going to be very tough. A large lump began to form in my throat.

I knew for sure that Kippy was sharing my heartfelt emotions. He stared at me solemnly and finally spoke. "If ya ain't gonna take it with you, kin I have yer electric train?"

My father had no trouble selling the house, mainly due to his asking price—$2500. A bargain, even in 1944.

The packing process then shifted into high gear. In the following weeks we swam in a sea of boxes and crates. My father prowled the Ishpeming alleys behind the stores, picking up every empty cardboard box he could lay his hands on. My mother filled them up as fast as he brought them home. She made instant decisions on what to take with us, what to give away, and what to throw away. This often led to sharp words.

"That's my favorite coffee cup," the old man cried indignantly.

My mother thrust the cup up to his face. "Have you taken a good look at your coffee cup lately? It's got a bigger crack than the Liberty Bell. I'm surprised it still *holds* coffee." She opened the cupboard above the kitchen sink. "In fact, I'm throwing out *all* of these old cups. And the glasses, too."

"Glasses" was a misnomer. Each time we polished off a jar of jelly the jar became a drinking glass. My mother faithfully stayed with the same brand at the A&P in order to collect a matching set, which now numbered twenty-seven. Peanut-butter jars were also saved, but they weren't our top-of-the-line glassware because they had a threaded lip for the screw-top.

The only crockery that survived the purge and were packed for the Milwaukee trip was my mother's treasured collection of Jewel Tea dishes. For years, every time the Jewel Tea home salesman pulled up in his panel truck, she acquired a piece of the Autumn Leaf pattern dishware: a cup here, a saucer there, or on special occasions a teapot or a gravy boat. None of the family were ever allowed to drink from a Jewel Tea cup or eat from a Jewel Tea plate. That stuff was strictly reserved for high-state functions like meetings of the Ishpeming Bethel Lutheran Women's Circle.

Relatives, friends, and neighbors glommed onto our furniture. Since everyone was equally needy, my parents didn't have the heart to charge them much. We quickly got rid of most of it, but the old man refused to part with his cherished floor-model Zenith radio. He lovingly placed it in a wooden crate and stuffed long underwear inside the cabinet to keep the tubes from breaking.

I had my own problems. Because my valuable collection of hand-built model airplanes was too large and too fragile to pack, I couldn't take them to Milwaukee. The Dauntless dive bomber—a crucial weapon in the Battle of Midway—was one model in particular that I couldn't bear to leave behind. I offered to hold the plane on my lap during the train ride, but because it was made of balsa wood and tissue paper and had a wing span of four feet, my mother vetoed the idea. I gave the airplane to Kippy.

However, Kippy didn't get my electric train for the simple reason that my Uncle Hugo wanted it. Family blood runs thicker than friend's blood.

A black man in a starched white jacket entered the train coach. "Lunch is being served in the dining car," he announced in a very regal voice.

I eagerly looked over at my mother sitting next to my old man across the aisle. "Kin we have lunch in the dining car?"

My mother looked at me like I'd lost my mind. She dipped into a large shopping bag and hauled out a catsup-laden Spam sandwich and thrust it at me. "We're not spending good money in dining cars. Here's your lunch."

This wasn't the first time I'd ridden on a train. When I was eight years old the old man had dipped into the kitchen sugar bowl, grabbed a handful of dollar bills from our savings, and went off on a week-long bender which he was inclined to do every couple of years or so. My mother decided that two could play at that frivolous-spending game, so she bought tickets for the two of us to take the 400 streamliner to Negaunee to see a first-run Jack Benny movie. I'd been really excited about the train ride until I found out that on the three-mile run from Ishpeming to Negaunee the streamliner didn't even get out of first gear.

But this time it was different. Milwaukee was three hundred miles from Ishpeming, and as the train neared the Wisconsin border, we were really clipping along. The telephone poles were whizzing by like a picket fence.

"I don't have nuthin' to drink with the sandwich," I told my mother.

She reached back into the bag, pulled out a thermos, and handed it to me. "It's milk."

I ate the sandwich and drank the milk. "Now can I go to the dining car and get some dessert?"

My mother reached into the shopping bag once again and brought out a thick slice of jelly roll.

The conductor marched through the coach announcing the next stop. "Oconto . . . Oconto, Wisconsin."

We had just crossed the state line. It was the first time I'd ever been out of Upper Michigan. I pressed my face up against the coach window and watched the foreign Wisconsin landscape pass by.

Uncle Bill Buffey stood and stared at our formidable array of cardboard boxes, wooden crates, and old suitcases sitting on the Milwaukee train-station platform. "Gawdalmighty, we're gonna have to make two trips."

Buffey, Aunt Martha, and my cousin Karen had moved to Milwaukee a few years back, and Uncle Bill had driven down to the train station to pick us up. We were going to stay with them until we found a place to live.

While Uncle Bill and my father tied down several of the boxes to the roof of the Buffey car I watched the bustle of activity at the railway station. There were many black people there, and I couldn't help but stare. Pretty soon some were looking back at me, curious to know what my problem was.

"Quit gawking at them or you're going to start something." my mother snapped.

The car was finally loaded with luggage, and we took off. Buffey drove down Wisconsin Avenue, the major Milwaukee thoroughfare.

I'd never seen anything like it. In each block there was at least one movie theater. Many were showing technicolor films. One of the theaters featured nothing but newsreels all day long. Cars were buzzing every which way, weaving around concrete traffic islands where clusters of people waited for street cars. High above the street were webs of power lines for the buses and streetcars.

There were several ten or twelve-story skyscrapers in every block, something I'd only seen in the movies. My father, of course, had already been in downtown Milwaukee on his job-hunting trip and was acting like a big-shot guide. "That's the Schroeder Hotel," he announced, pointing to the tallest building. "Got a coffee shop on the ground floor. One a these days we'll go in fer coffee and donuts."

My mother scoffed at that, knowing that you just didn't walk into a big hotel for coffee and donuts.

Uncle Bill proceeded up Wisconsin Avenue, leaving the

downtown district behind. I rolled down the rear window and stuck my head out in the frigid air to get one last look at the Milwaukee skyline.

A few days later our family was in our new home, such as it was. We were the proud tenants of a third-floor walk-up in a converted old Victorian house on Eighteenth Street. It had one bedroom, a kitchenette area, and a tiny living room. The community bathroom was down the hall. The rooms were cluttered with deeply scratched, heavy old furniture. A mismatched pair of overstuffed chairs had threadbare cushions. The ancient refrigerator made an ominous, clanking sound.

I gazed around. "Can't we find a better place?"

"It's close to where Pop will be working," my mother said. "And there's a school just three blocks away."

"Where do I sleep?" I asked.

The old man brushed back a floor-length curtain on one living-room wall and pulled down a bed that had been folded up into a small closet.

"It's a Murphy bed," he explained.

I knew all about Murphy beds. I'd seen them in movies with the Three Stooges, and the beds were notorious for suddenly folding up into the closet any time someone lay down on them. It was hilarious on film, but in real life I wanted none of it.

"I ain't sleeping on that thing," I said.

The old man had seen the same movies and hefted the foot rail of the bed up and down off the floor. "Look here, ya really haf'ta pull it up hard to get it back into the closet. Ain't no way it'll fold up by itself. Get on an' try it out."

"I ain't gettin' on that bed."

"Go 'head, try it. Ain't gonna bite ya."

"Uh-uh."

"C'mon. Try it."

Against my better judgement I agreed to try the Murphy bed. I nervously lay there, staring at the ceiling. Sure enough, the foot of the bed began rising off the floor. I watched my feet going up, and I started yelling bloody murder. Grinning, my father slowly lowered the foot of the bed back to the floor.

"Quit fooling around, or he'll be wanting to sleep with us," my mother told him. "And you've seen the size of *that* bed."

The next day my father started his job at International Harvester, and my mother decided to go shopping at the downtown Gimbels department store to replace, among other things, the jelly-jar glasses we'd left behind. I didn't have to register at the new school until the following day so my mother took me along to help carry packages. I wanted to take the bus downtown, but she said that the nickel bus fares could be used for better things, so we walked the sixteen blocks to Gimbels.

As we neared the downtown area, I couldn't help gawking up at the tall buildings. My mother grabbed me by the collar saying, "Quit that. People will think we're from the sticks."

We *were* from the sticks, of course, but she didn't want to advertise it.

We soon found that big-city shopping required real dexterity and steady nerves. For example, Gimbels had the trickiest door I'd ever seen. My mother hadn't seen anything like it either, and we both stood outside the store looking at it. People were walking into this big glass cylinder containing four inside panes that were whirling madly around. Somehow everyone was getting in and out of the store by stepping quickly between these panes, walking in a half circle, and then stepping out.

"Should we try it?" I asked.

"You first," my mother said.

I cautiously stepped up, carefully trying to avoid the people who were being spit out of the store through the same door. Everyone using it, going both in and out, looked unconcerned, nonchalantly stepping between the revolving glass panes to get to the other side. But I could see that it wasn't that simple. If you didn't time your entrance perfectly or took one misstep, the door could pin an arm or a leg and easily whack it off.

I waited until no one was using the strange door and hopped in. I'd no sooner got between two of the panes when the door slid to a stop. I was halfway in and halfway out, alone, and trapped in a glass prison. Panic-stricken, I looked out at my mother who was standing safely out on the sidewalk. She shrugged at me.

Finally, the door began to move again. A woman with an armload of packages on the other side of the door was pushing to get out, at the same time eyeing me suspiciously.

You have to push it, I realized. I gave the pane in front of me a shove and walked around, only to find myself back out on the sidewalk next to my mother.

"I don't think you've got the hang of it yet," she said.

We studied it further and then, hand in hand, leapt into one of the pie-shaped slots in the door. It seemed somewhat crowded with two of us in the same slot, but at least we managed to get into the store.

Gimbels was huge, with dozens upon dozens of counters and display cases, and that was only the ground floor. My mother quickly scoped it out and said, "I think the housewares must be on another floor. Do you see the stairs?"

I pointed toward the center of the store where I saw people

going up to the second floor. Except they weren't walking up stairs. They were just standing, and the stairs were moving, taking them upward. It was the first escalator I'd ever seen.

But it didn't look too difficult to me since even old women my mother's age were casually stepping on and away they went, up toward the ceiling.

I had to try it, so I eagerly stepped onto the moving stairway. Right off the bat I found that, like the devilish whirling door, it required precise eye-foot coordination. A metal step formed right beneath my shoes, and for a split second only my toes were perched on the edge of the step. I stumbled backward and luckily grabbed the moving handrail to keep from breaking my neck. I shouted a warning to my mother who was about to get on.

"Watch where you step, Ma. It's tricky."

We arrived on the second floor and discovered that housewares were on the third floor. Another ride on moving stairs.

While my mother was picking out cups and glasses I found the down escalator, jumped on, and rode down a floor. Then back up and back down again. After I'd done this several times a man in a dark suit and a nameplate on his breast tapped me on the shoulder.

"Young man, are you in the store with an adult?"

"I'm ten years old, sir," I replied righteously. "Almost eleven."

But he just stood there, waiting for a different answer, so I trotted off in search of my mother.

Later that afternoon I was outside our apartment, test-flying my newly built balsa glider when the kid who lived next door got home from school. Wally Schultz was nine years old, and after he inspected my glider we began talking about model airplanes. It was immediately apparent than he was a rank amateur in the field.

"I'm workin' on a P-38," Wally said.

"Oh? Flying model or solid?" I asked.

"Whut?"

"Is it a model that can fly or one you carve from balsa blocks?"

"Well, it's got sheets of wood with millions of little pieces on them that you have to cut out and glue together. An' the whole thing gets covered with tissue paper."

"That's a flying model."

"It's my first one," Wally admitted. "Ain't really got started on it yet. It looks hard."

"Yeah. A P-38's got twin engines. Mebbe you should'a started on a Spitfire or a Flying Tiger. They only got one engine and are easier to build."

My expertise on the subject impressed Wally. "How would'ja like to come over an' look at it? I need some help."

"Sure."

"Why don'cha come over for dinner?" Wally suggested. "We always got lots to eat."

I went up and told my mother that I'd been invited over to dinner.

"Did his mother say it was okay?" she wanted to know.

"I only talked to Wally, but he said they always got lots to eat."

"Well, you go over there and see if it's okay with his mother."

"It's just about time to go anyway. Wally sez they eat early."

"At least change your pants," she said.

I put on my church-going pants and went next door. The Schultz family must have been in the bucks because they lived in a ground-floor apartment much larger than ours. Wally introduced me to his mother, a jolly, roly-poly woman who declared that I was more than welcome to have dinner with them. Wally had a seven-year-old sister, Lucy, who didn't have much to say but giggled a lot.

Mrs. Schultz kept glancing at the wall clock. At thirteen minutes past five she bolted into the kitchen and hurriedly began bringing out steaming plates of food to the dining-room table. Wally's father was nowhere to be seen. But precisely at five-fifteen the front door suddenly opened and Mr. Schultz made his entrance.

Schultz was a barrel-chested man with a chin that jutted out an incredible distance and close-cropped blonde hair without sideburns.

Without a word Schultz sat down at the head of the table and began loading up a plate with food. But it wasn't for himself; he passed it across the table to Mrs. Schultz and then immediately began filling another one for Wally's sister. I looked at her loaded plate thinking that there was no way a little girl could eat that much. I would be proven wrong.

Next, Schultz made a plate for Wally, and only then did he notice my presence at the table.

"This is Wally's friend, Jerry," Mrs. Schultz told her husband. "They just moved in next door."

Schultz nodded curtly, staring at me while he mentally estimated my body mass. After determining how much I should be able to eat, he handed me a plate heaped high with sauerkraut, potato pancakes, thick slices of black bread, and large, aromatic sausages which I found out later were bratwurst.

Schultz then produced a gigantic bottle of Blatz and began pouring for everyone. A glass of beer with a foaming head landed in front of me.

"Uh, sir, I don't think I should drink that."

Schultz looked at me with impatient surprise and spoke for the first time. "Vhy not?" he asked in a thick German accent.

"Uh, my mother wouldn't like it."

Schultz raised his eyebrows at the notion that a female could influence anyone's decisions. "Efferybody drinks beer. It's gud for you, luts uf vitamins."

"Mr. Schultz works at the Blatz brewery," Mrs. Schultz explained.

"I been drinking beer ever since I kin remember," Wally chimed in. "So does Lucy."

Lucy took a sip of her Blatz and giggled. Maybe beer was the reason she giggled all the time. I idly wondered if the Schultz household served beer with breakfast and lunch as well.

As far as Mr. Schultz was concerned, the subject was closed. He took his knife and fork and started to saw up his bratwurst. This was the signal for everyone to begin eating.

I'd never had sauerkraut before. It tasted terrible. I took a sip of beer to wash down the sauerkraut and couldn't decide which tasted worse, the sauerkraut or the beer. To this day I still hate sauerkraut, but in later years I've revised my opinion about the taste of beer.

Schultz kept glancing over at my glass of beer so I self-consciously finished it off with the meal. When I put down the empty glass, Schultz then said to me, "Dot's all der beer you get—vun glass. Ve don't vant any drunks in zis house."

After dinner I gave Wally a few pointers on assembling his P-38 model and then went home, feeling unwell. My stomach was in fierce conflict with the bratwurst, sauerkraut, potato pancakes, and beer. Large bubbles of noxious gas were drifting up my esophagus, resulting in resonant, foul-tasting belches. I burped magnificently just as I walked into our apartment.

"What's that smell?" my mother asked.

"It's sauerkraut," I said.

But my mother had the nose of a bloodhound. "There's another smell." She leaned over me. "It's beer. You've been drinking beer." She'd had a lot of experience with the smell of beer whenever my old man came home after one of his benders.

"Wally's father gave it to me, honest. Only one glass. They all drink beer at supper. Even Wally's seven-year-old sister."

"Seven-year-olds drinking beer?" My mother looked at me incredulously. Finally, she decided that the story was so preposterous that it must have been true. "That's the last time you're going over there for supper, or any other meal."

"That's okay with me. I hate sauerkraut."

And that was my introduction to big-city life. The next day I entered the fifth grade at Kilbourn Grade School. Milwaukee schools were unbelievably easy. My new classmates were struggling over things I'd already learned in the U.P. The teachers were kind and gentle, unlike the tyrants I'd served under at Central Grade School in Ishpeming. I joined the school Safety Cadets and got to wear a white Sam Browne belt and a fancy badge. School kids couldn't cross the street until I waved them on. I adapted readily to this new position of power.

I frequented the Milwaukee Museum where I discovered real, honest-to-gawd Egyptian mummies which I would visit many times.

I became an expert on the Milwaukee public transit system. For five cents I could ride around the city for hours, using a free-transfer slip to switch buses and street cars. There wasn't a place in the city I couldn't find.

Using revolving doors and escalators became routine.

But I still didn't believe we'd be living in Milwaukee very long and wrote a letter to Kippy, telling him that I'd see him soon. This was not to be. In 1947 we moved back to the U.P. but lived in Republic, and I lost touch with Kippy. I didn't see him again for almost 50 years, after we had both achieved senior-citizen status. Again, we've become the best of friends.

Biography

Jerry Harju was born in Ishpeming, Michigan, in 1933. He received a degree in engineering from the University of Michigan in 1957 and an M.S. from the University of Southern California in 1985. After thirty years as a manager in the aerospace industry in Southern California, Jerry began writing as a second career. His first three books, *Northern Reflections, Northern D'Lights, Northern Passages*, and his latest, *Northern Memories*, are collections of humorous short stories about growing up in the Upper Peninsula in the 1930's and '40's. *The Class of '57* takes readers along a humorous and nostalgic path during Harju's six years of "higher education" at the University of Michigan. University life then—with its 1950's attitudes on world affairs, morality, and women's roles in society—was much different from today. *Cold Cash* is Jerry's first novel, a wacky tale about two amateurs who decide to solve their cash-flow problems by pulling a bank heist and getting away on snowmobiles. Typical of Harju's work, the robbery doesn't go as planned and is further complicated by two strong-willed women. The book won a Midwest Independent Publishers Association Book Achievement Award in 1999. *Here's what I think...* is a collection of Jerry's columns that have appeared for the past several years in the Marquette newspaper, the *Mining Journal*. Jerry received the 2000 U.P. Writer of the Year award for this effort.

In addition to writing books and newspaper and magazine columns and running a publishing company, Jerry travels all over the globe.